The Korean War and Me

A Memoir by Ted Pailet

iUniverse, Inc.
New York Lincoln Shanghai

The Korean War and Me

iUniverse books may be ordered through booksellers or by contacting:

iUniverse
2021 Pine Lake Road, Suite 100
Lincoln, NE 68512
www.iuniverse.com
1-800-Authors (1-800-288-4677)

ISBN: 0-595-33433-4 (pbk)
ISBN: 0-595-66926-3 (cloth)

Printed in the United States of America

The Korean War and Me

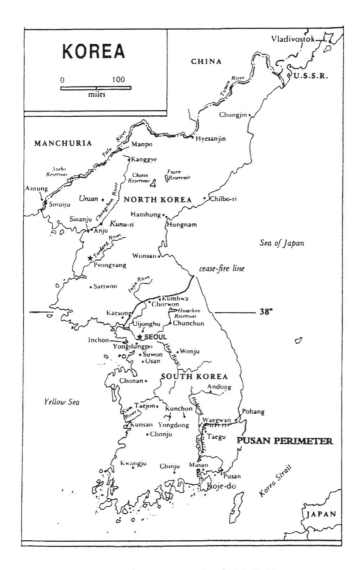

Figure 1—The Korean Peninsula 1953–1954

Contents

Introduction, Acknowledgements & Dedication

The featured guest speaker at my high school graduation exercise (to the best of my memory) said, among other things, "You have concluded the most impressionable years of your lives. The events you have thus far experienced and the associations to which you have been exposed have shaped your attitudes and your character and have formed your value system. *You* are now *you*. From now on it's a matter of maturation."

Perhaps—but I'm not so sure.

In my case, I am certain that my tour of duty in Korea (1953–1954) did more than mature my characteristics. The experience has had such a profound affect on me—I think a somewhat more-than-expected transformation took place. The Army taught me the principles of leadership and gave me the opportunity to practice what I learned. The Army put me into a position of responsibility for men and equipment. In Korea, I faced the horrors of war and dealt with life and death situations. My assignments forced me to self-start, to take the initiative, and they helped prepare me for the inevitable challenges of life. I believe the skills I acquired gave me an advantage in my subsequent business, professional, civic and religious involvements.

During my tour I took many 35 mm color slides. They are pretty good, and I have kept them all. However, despite what they say about a picture being worth a thousand words, in my opinion, pictures cannot convey this story as well as the written word. Plus, sitting through the showing of 300 slides is boring, impractical, and valueless without my explaining each slide and what was going on at the time. Instead, I have embedded 50 of the most relevant and illustrative images into the text of this work. They are black and white instead of color, for the sake of clarity. I also re-read all of the letters I wrote to Louise. She had saved them, and they provided a wealth of detail that aided me in this work. Throughout the text, I quote conversations. Obviously, these quotes reflect the "best of my memory" and not the exact words spoken.

As far as the historical facts and statistics that appear throughout the text, many were available to me in the letters and other materials I mailed to Louise, like copies of *The Stars and Stripes, Korean Edition.* I have read several accounts of the Korean War, like *This Kind of War,* by General Matthew Ridgeway. Also, my memory benefited greatly from reading *A Brief Account of the Korean War, 50th Anniversary Commemorative Edition,* written by Jack D. Walker and published by the Korean War Association in Nashville.

Up until very recently, thanks to the computer and the word processor, there was no practical way for me to get this story on paper, much less to include embedded images that relate to the text. I was, therefore, driven by two desires: one, to learn word-processing, and two, to preserve the story for my progeny. In the event that those who come after me should read this story, my hope is that they will get to know me as I was then, will acquire an understanding of what life was like in the early 1950s, and perhaps find some of it helpful in living their own lives. I wish my forbearers had shared their story with me.

Fifty years is a long time. Happily, many of the people who played roles in this narrative have read early drafts of some or all of the chapters. These include Harry Martin, Joe Bernstein, Albert Mintz, Fred Rosenberg and Ann Silberman. Others, like their spouses and good friends, helped convince me that I seemed to be doing something of interest. Their encouragement played a large part in stimulating the motivation it takes (for me) to find the time to write.

I learned long ago that when it comes to writing, I am error prone. Furthermore, my spelling is "at troches." My son, Al, is the opposite. For his expert proofreading and attention to detail I am forever grateful. I am also grateful for his keen sensitivity in what is currently referred to as "PC." or Political Correctness. In an early draft, he pointed out certain passages of mine that would offend today's (much less a future) reader, despite how acceptable it may have been during the 1940s and 50s. Following his advice, I did soften some of those passages.

On the other hand, my good friend David Popkin, who is a university professor, points out that if he had to adhere to current political correctness, he wouldn't be able to teach American or English literature—including *Huckleberry Finn.* He was an early advisor and ongoing proofreader-critic. He provided valuable suggestions which helped keep me focused and improve clarity.

In large part this is my story, but in a more significant sense it is "our" story. Louise was a definite partner in getting us through those days. Figuratively speaking, she never left my side, and I always knew she was with me all the way.

During the writing of this memoir I showed Louise a draft of each chapter. Thanks to *her* memory, she revised names and events I thought for sure were correct. Plus, she found misspellings and wrong word usage that even the word processor missed.

With love and devotion I dedicate this work to Louise; but for her it never would have happened. And I wish to make a special dedication to Jacques L'Blanc, who symbolizes the many GI's now known (sadly) as MIA's, some of whom will never be found…

1

Ready or Not, Here I Go!

2ⁿᵈ Lt. Theodore H. Pailet, USAR #0-2004577—You are ordered to report to Fort Lewis, Washington on February 15, 1953 for assignment to the Far East Command.
Louise and I went into shock. I don't know why; we knew I wouldn't be lucky enough to get one of my three choices: 1st) Caribbean, 2nd) Europe, 3rd) Hawaii. This meant I'd be going to war—joining the brutal fighting that had been raging in Korea for two and a half years. It meant being separated from Louise for at least a year and sent to the unknown on the opposite side of the world. "Maybe," I fantasized, "just maybe they'll assign me to duty in Japan or some island like Guam or Okinawa." I replied to myself, "Don't get your hopes up!" That gave us fourteen days to wind things up and for me to fly out to Tacoma, Washington.

Doggone it; there I was, enjoying a super assignment as Commissary Officer at Fort Monmouth, New Jersey. Actually, my assignment out of the Quartermaster Corps' Officer's Training School at Fort Lee, VA was Assistant Commissary Officer. I figured I got that assignment because I had received a Bachelor of Science degree in Commerce and Business Administration at the University of Alabama. However, shortly after I reported, my boss Captain Wells suffered a heart attack and I was elevated to his office as Acting Commissary Officer. Fortunately, I had an experienced civilian manager named Joey Palermo. What a great job! I was twenty-three years old and the head of a busy supermarket. The local vendors showered me with samples: fresh eggs (double yolk), fresh produce of all descriptions, bakery goods (still hot), and a different surprise every day or so: trying to entice me to carry their products. There were many truck farms nearby and we had the authority to purchase fresh produce, as well as bakery and dairy products locally. Everything else—the non-perishables—came from the 1ˢᵗ Army central distribution facilities.

Fort Monmouth was the Army's Signal Corps Headquarters. Lots of top-secret research and development was going on there. Bell operated five large laboratories. The transistor was developed in one of those laboratories. It was also where Senator Joseph McCarthy hunted for "Communist Pinkos" who may have infiltrated the laboratories. I'll never forget the commanding general. He was an absolute fanatic on the subject of safety. His favorite saying, "There is no such thing as an accident—it is premeditated negligence!" was painted on a bold-lettered sign about every 100 yards all over the post. God help you if you ever had an accident! If you did, you had to report directly to him in his office for a royal chewing-out. The general's favorite saying is permanently engraved somewhere in my brain.

My daily routine began by reporting to the Quartermaster Corps (QMC) base unit headquarters for reveille at 0600 hours. We were led in the Daily Dozen (twelve different calisthenics) by some loud-barking drill sergeant, then we listened to announcements. After being dismissed from that formation, 5 or 6 of us would pile into someone's car, go to a little off-post diner for coffee and freshly grilled English Muffins with lots of homemade butter. From there it was off to work at the Post Commissary.

Louise and I had only been married a little over 16 months. We drove a green 1950 Chevy and rented a tiny but comfortable apartment in Eatontown, NJ. Our apartment was next to the Monmouth Race Track and walking distance to the Commissary. As a 2nd Lieutenant I was making $333.00 a month. That may not seem like much, but somehow during the eight months we spent at Fort Monmouth we managed to go somewhere nice almost every weekend. A couple of the highlights were the Army-Navy Game In Philadelphia for Thanksgiving (lobster at Ye Ole Bookbinders) and a trip to Louise's cousins in Westchester County for Christmas. (Both were born and raised Jewish—Lewis Solomon and Jane Sternheimer—but now were Lewis and Jane Stanton: Congregationalists.)

That Rosh Hashanah we went to services at a synagogue not far from Eatontown. After services, a dignified, older couple named Erlanger approached and invited us to their home in Deal, an upscale residential community on the Jersey coast near Asbury Park. The home was gorgeous. It was nestled amongst a thicket of trees and featured an aviary. Mr. Erlanger was thrilled to give us the grand tour as he identified each of his many birds. Meanwhile, Mrs. Erlanger prepared "tea." They were from England originally, and were very British. They insisted we join them at their home after Yom Kippur for "Break-Fast"—the kind of couple one never forgets.

By the way, Louise's cousin, Lewis Stanton, had a brother named Bernard M. Stanton, and two sisters: Bernice (Solomon) Mohr and Jeanne (Solomon) Rosenberg. Only the two brothers changed their names and religion. When I was attending Officers' Training School at Fort Lee, VA., B.M. (sorry, but that's what everybody called him) invited Louise and me to visit him and his family. B.M. had become a Presbyterian and his wife was Roman Catholic. They lived in Virginia Beach in a lovely home facing the ocean. B.M. was a successful business-man. He had accumulated quite a few parking lots in Virginia Beach and Norfolk and served as president of the National Parking Association. He and his wife insisted upon taking us to the Cavalier Beach Club for dinner, despite the fact that the club was restricted against Jews, even as guests. Furthermore, the Stan-ton's arranged to let us have guest privileges whenever we wanted to use the club. It was by far the most desirable facility along Virginia Beach.

We particularly enjoyed mid-town Manhattan. It was easy to get to by com-muter train and was affordable, provided I wore my uniform (even better, since I was an officer). The train fare was fifty cents from the Red Bank Station to Penn Station. The New Yorker Hotel, connected to Penn station, charged service men in uniform only $7.00 a night. Typically, after we checked into the hotel we would walk to Mama Leone's, our favorite restaurant. It was in the heart of the Broadway Theater District. There was always a line waiting to get in, but the man at the door would proudly usher us right in because I was in an officer's uni-form. This was done with the obvious, unanimous approval of those in line ahead of us. The minute we sat down, they served a large relish tray with everything in it of the best quality—along with a basket loaded with breads and rolls right out of the oven. This was new to us. We were used to saltine crackers, Melba toast, French or corn bread. The choice of food was extensive—all delicious and all memorable. After dinner we would stroll around and decide what show to see ("South Pacific," "The King and I," "Where the Boys Are," among many) or what show we could get tickets for at the last minute.

There was so much else to enjoy: Radio City Music Hall, with its large-screen movie and live stage entertainment featuring the Rockettes, window shopping along Fifth Avenue, The Monkey Bar when we could afford a supper club, and meeting friends. We met our friends under the clock in the lobby of the Biltmore Hotel, the customary meeting place for our age group. In fact we could just go there and before long someone we knew would show up. Usually we would go to the cocktail lounge, have drinks, smoke cigarettes, exchange stories, and gossip. It was quite a challenge keeping up with college friends. After graduation we were all moving around like crazy, with service in the military dominating everyone's plans.

Louise's mother and dad met us in New York one weekend. Her dad was a homebuilder-developer and built tract housing under the FHA and VA programs. He wanted to see Levittown—a highly publicized, 1,000 acre, 17,000-new-home-development. While Louise and her mother shopped, he and I took the train twenty-five miles out on Long Island to see the operation and the furnished models. He was fascinated; he related to the professionalism required for such a huge undertaking on what was nothing but potato farms. I didn't understand all the behind-the-scenes effort like he did, but I was extremely impressed with what I saw.

Louise, being very personable, had the ability to make friends quickly and easily. For example, she went to a luncheon hosted by the general's wife to welcome the wives of newly arrived officers. In two minutes she was on a first name basis and knew their life's history. Still, it was amazing how fast we became close to some of our contemporaries at Monmouth. Jean and 1st Lt. John Adams were from east Tennessee. She was pregnant when we met, and she delivered (free but natural) in the post infirmary. Immediately after the delivery, they rolled her and the baby back to her bed in the open, crowded maternity ward and plopped a stack of linens at the foot of her bed. "Honey, here are your clean sheets and towels, whenever you're up to it. The orderly will pick up the dirty ones." Louise, Carolyn & 2nd Lt. Clark Biggs, our other close friends, and I were not permitted to stay and help because of the maternity ward rules. It amazed us how well Jean and the baby got along and how fast they were back in their apartment. The Biggs' were from Conway, AK and were a real fun couple to be with.

When Louise and I found out that the 1952 presidential election campaign was going to be televised, we bought a TV set. Thanks to John Adams and his Signal Corps training, he was able to rig up an antenna to pick up the TV signal from the tower in New York. We selected a Dumont. It had a small round screen, a lousy picture, lots of snow, and the screen would start rolling over for no reason whatsoever. It was still an awesome treat to be able to watch Adlai Stevenson and Dwight Eisenhower deliver their campaign speeches. I liked Stevenson because of his vision and his sense of humor. To me, Eisenhower had been in the army too long. We were also fascinated at being able to see shows like Ed Sullivan, Sid Caesar, Victor Borge, and watch live baseball games being played in Yankee Stadium or Ebbets Field 50 miles away. There were just a few daytime shows: Bob and Ray with their clever antics, and a new young comedian named Jack Lemmon. There were only three channels. Most of the time all we had were Test Patterns.

◆   ◆   ◆

Joey Palermo was a good commissary manager—full of personality. One day he fired a cashier on the spot. You've never heard such screaming! She had a broom leaning against her checkout counter. He accused her of adding the price of the broom to unwary customers' checks and pocketing the money. No telling how many times she "sold" that broom or how many other tricks the cashiers had. We had an antiquated, mostly manual control system. As far as the Army was concerned, our mission was to offer a reasonably good selection of groceries, meats, produce and household items at as low a price as we could to break even.

On the side, Joey also managed rental property. He tried to high-pressure me into buying one of the new subdivision homes being built in Monmouth County. The idea was that I would buy the home with a no-money-down 100% GI loan. He would manage it; keep it rented for enough to make the monthly payments, a commission for himself, and a profit for me while I was overseas. When I got back, I would sell it and make a lot of money. I didn't do the deal—bad mistake—but who knows?

As the time approached for my departure, we started doing "last time" things. Captain Wells had recovered from his heart attack but was still puny and on limited duty. He and Joey gave us a surprise going away party at the Commissary. They invited all of the employees and all of our friends. It turned out to be very emotional. Everyone seemed to know someone serving in Korea, so it was, "Here's his name. Should you run into him, tell him I said hello." Or "Good luck, and if you get a chance, let us hear from you." Some tried to be funny; "The longer you're over there the whiter they get." And the favorite cliché, "Let us know if it's true that it runs sideways,"—references, of course, to the anatomy of Asian women.

We spent our last weekend in Manhattan. Our long-time friend Joe Bernstein had recently been assigned to Fort Monmouth after Fort Lee. He and I grew up in New Orleans; both of us attended Tulane, transferred to the University of Alabama and were in the ROTC (Reserve Officers Training Corps) when the Korean War began. He was still single. Louise got him a date with Beth Isaacs, a friend with whom she had grown up in Nashville. Beth was studying dance in New York. The four of us had a farewell dinner at Mama Leone's, and then we went to see "The King and I." During the show my mind was elsewhere, but the lyrics to one of the songs caught my attention: "Whenever I feel afraid/I hold my head up high/and whistle a happy tune/then no one else will know I'm afraid."

◆   ◆   ◆

The car was loaded. The TV was sticking out of the trunk, with the lid tied to the bumper. The cab was jam-packed with everything we had not already shipped to Nashville. On our drive up to Fort Monmouth, the route was Knoxville, Roanoke, Richmond, Washington, Baltimore, Philadelphia and then Eatontown. In order to see a different part of the country, we drove the New Jersey Turnpike to Pittsburgh, then to Columbus, Cincinnati, Louisville, and Nashville. We visited with Louise's mother, dad and grandmother "Tuts," and had more emotional good-byes. Tuts sobbed for fear I would never see her again because of her advanced age. One of their friends, Dr. Weinstein, gave me money and a shopping list, just in case I was in Japan and had some extra time. He was a collector and wanted certain hand-carved ivory figurines. Then we flew to New Orleans to say farewell to my mother, dad, brother and friends before I left for Fort Lewis. My dad was a jeweler. His store—Pailet & Penedo—not only served New Orleaneans on a retail basis but provided jewelry repair service to small stores in the surrounding area. In addition to retail and repair services, he manufactured customized jewelry in his shop. Customers were always lined up, waiting for his personalized attention. He gave me a crash course in cultured pearls just in case I had the opportunity to make a contact in Japan. My mother, bless her, had total faith in God. She just knew that everything was for the best and that I would be fine. My brother Lester was a freshman at Tulane, but he did not let that interfere with his social life; he loved to party. Actually, he was in the process of transferring to The Parsons School of Design in New York City, which was better suited to his artistic gifts. He spent every possible moment with Louise and me throughout our visit. Situations like that are difficult for everyone. What can be said? Most said "Take good care of yourself." My Dad drove Louise and me to the airport. As he kissed me good-bye, he stuck a wad of cash in my pocket, and then waited in the car while Louise walked with me to the gate to hug, kiss and say our farewells.

Awesome…mixed emotions…a head full of questions as I gazed down at the western states and the snow-capped peaks of the Rocky Mountains passing below. What was it going to be like? How would I hold up? How would I handle the separation from Louise? What about my mother, dad and brother? Sure, they all put on a good front for my sake, but what was really going on inside? Was it anything like what was going on inside me? These thoughts were colliding against my spirit of adventure. It was a sensation like being in a free-fall.

Boy, was I ever processed for overseas duty! Have you ever seen pictures of a long line of nude soldiers going through an assembly line physical exam? That's how the Army treated the enlisted men. Thankfully, they treated officers with a bit more dignity. We were ushered from station to station. I couldn't even begin to count the stations, much less the many inoculations. Whoopee, I passed! The joke was "If you want to get discharged real quickly, while the doctor is checking you for a hernia just lean over and kiss him on the back of his neck." Next was issuance of all the appropriate clothing. Everything had to fit in one foot locker, one duffle bag, and one carry-on. After the processing, every morning we had to search for our name on the various lists posted on a huge bulletin board—listed alphabetically by troop ship or flight passenger lists. If your name did not appear on any of the lists you were free to leave the post as long as you returned by curfew. There wasn't that much to do other than write letters or go into downtown Tacoma. Oh, and try to get a glimpse of Mt. Rainier through the overcast skies. I remember seeing one movie there: *I Love Melville,* starring Donald O' Conner and Debbie Reynolds.

Suddenly, panic struck. Reports of a weapon and ammunition shortage in Korea began to appear in the papers and on the radio. Rumors circulated like crazy. GI's swarmed Tacoma and even Seattle to buy any kind of firearm, knife, even brass knuckles, they could find. They emptied every store and pawnshop. As scary as it was to witness, I did not participate. I don't know exactly why. I guess I couldn't picture myself in a combat situation. Maybe I had enough confidence in the U.S. Army to correct any shortage before I got there. After all, I figured, it would take more than two weeks to cross the Pacific Ocean by troop ship and to get assigned to a unit. Regardless, it was one more thing to worry about.

After six days of this, my name appeared on a list. I couldn't believe it! Mine was one of just eight names (all officers) on a flight list. There were four Medical Corps officers (two majors and two captains), three Artillery Corps second lieutenants and me. The majors had served in World War II and were still in the Reserves. The Medical Corps captains were allowed to complete their medical training (rather than be drafted), but in exchange they had to serve in the Reserves for a minimum of two years.

In Korea, the fighting was at a pretty high pitch. The opposing armies were advancing and retreating, hill by hill. Names like "Heartbreak Ridge" and "Pork Chop Hill" became famous for the gruesome amount of blood spilled on those valueless slopes. There were so many casualties that the army was calling up Medical Corps Reserve officers like mad, allowing practicing doctors just a week or so to report to Ft. Lewis. I could understand the hurry as far as the doctors were concerned. Also, there was a shortage of artillery officers, which I later found out, were being used as forward observers. The job of a forward observer was to sneak up (heavily camouflaged) in front of the lines until he could observe the enemy positions through his binoculars. Then, after every salvo he would redirect the artillery batteries with his walkie-talkie—"3-degrees to the left," "100 yards forward," and other calls like that. He had to move around frequently because as soon as the North Koreans figured out his position they would do everything they could to kill him. Not only that, but sometimes he would encounter an enemy sneaking up from the opposite direction with the same job! (Oy vey!) The casualty rate for forward observers was horrendous. You would think that forward observing would be the top assignment that no one in their right mind would want, but surprisingly, there were those who actually volunteered. Anyway, I could understand the Army sending over the doctors and the Artillery officers, but why me—a Business Administration major?

The eight of us reported to the departure area with our gear all packed and labeled. An army bus with a driver and a Transportation Officer were waiting for us. The officer introduced himself as Captain Swenson, and then barked out our names. As we identified ourselves, he handed each of us a packet. On the bus he announced, "I will be escorting you gentlemen to the Vancouver International Airport. You will be taking a Canadian Pacific Airline flight to the Far East Command Headquarters in Tokyo, Japan. Your orders and tickets are in the packet." In an effort to cheer us up, he told the joke about the two drunks walking along a railroad track. One turned to the other and said, "Jeez, this is the tallest flight of stairs I've ever seen!" The other drunk said, "It's not the stairs that are bothering me; it's these low hand rails."

We arrived in Vancouver early, so rather than going directly to the airport, Swenson had the driver give us a tour of this beautiful city. He showed us Stanley Park, its totem poles and gorgeous view of the harbor, with the city's skyline and snow-capped mountains for a backdrop. We still arrived at the airport with time to spare. It was the year of Queen Elizabeth's Coronation, so the airport's gift shop was loaded with souvenirs of the occasion. I bought English cookies packaged in a blue tin container, beautifully decorated to commemorate the big event, and sent it to Louise.

Swenson said, "Good luck gentlemen; God be with you" as we walked, single-file, out to board the plane…

2

What a Strange Culture

The plane was a Super DC-6 with four propeller-driven Rolls Royce engines. The pilot announced that we would be flying at an altitude of about 18,000 feet at a speed of 350 nautical miles an hour, and that the flying time to Anchorage, Alaska would be about eight hours, depending on the head winds. He told us to relax and enjoy the clear visibility, which was rare this time of the year in this part of the world. The plane was less than half filled with a strange assortment of passengers. In addition to the eight of us, there was a group of U.S. Army non-commissioned officers who had been on furlough and were returning to their units in Alaska and the Aleutian Islands. Then there was a small group of Canadian military who could very well be on their way to Korea. The civilians were a mixture: some looked like Eskimos; some looked like European or Asian businessmen. I sat next to and struck up a conversation with one of the doctors, a captain named Don. He was a mild mannered OB/GYN. The other captain was Ed, a young general practitioner. All of the doctors were easy to be with, but the Artillery lieutenants were cliquish. I did find out that they were graduates of Texas A&M, which was military oriented. The views of the Canadian and Alaskan coastline and snow-covered mountains were simply breathtaking. Watching the majestic, multi-colored sunset was one of those rare spiritual encounters.

It was dark and inhumanly cold when we landed. An Army bus took us to some drab facility where we could walk around, stretch and get something hot to eat. To and from the airport—which wasn't much more than a landing field—the bus passed though the center of Anchorage. It resembled a Wild West frontier town like you see in the cowboy movies—wooden sidewalks and muddy streets, saloons, dry goods and general stores, even an assayer's office. The temperature was somewhere around zero. It felt even colder to me because of the biting wind, especially on the walks to and from the bus.

After we reached cruising altitude, the pilot announced that in approximately eight hours we would land for refueling and servicing, but he revealed nothing else until we were crossing the International Date Line. He explained that it was now "tomorrow"—that is, on the East side of the line it was Sunday and on the West side of the line it was Monday. He advised us to try to get some sleep. I tried, but the ride was bumpy and it didn't take much to make me feel queasy. During this segment of the flight, Don and I were sitting a row behind two of the Artillery officers. I overheard them talking about forward observers. Then it hit me like a ton of bricks! "Oh, no! Why didn't I think of it earlier! Now I know why I am on this plane!" When I was at Alabama I was enrolled in the Quarter-master Corps ROTC (Reserve Officers Training Corps) program, but during my sophomore year I had to double-up in order to get all of my required ROTC credits. I had added a semester of the only course available to me: Artillery. My thoughts went wild with different scenarios, convincing myself that shortly I'd be a forward observer with my life expectancy reduced to a couple of days.

The pilot explained that we would be under strict security procedures during this stop. No cameras or any violation of orders would be tolerated. The window shades were closed. I got a quick glimpse of the landing strip as we went from the plane to the bus. The strip looked to me like it went from one end of a small island to the other. I didn't see anything else. So many of the passengers got off the plane in Anchorage that those of us who continued on the flight—including the two pilots, a navigator and two cute-looking Canadian stewardesses—fit into one bus. The bus ride lasted about 20 minutes. The whole time it felt as if the bus was descending along a winding driveway. When the bus stopped, we got out in what was obviously an underground living facility for military personnel. There were all sorts of U.S. Air Force, as well as some Engineering Corps commissioned and non-commissioned officers mulling around. We were allowed to buy any-thing at the cafeteria or PX, but we were told to stay together and to relax in the lounge, but not to engage in conversation with anyone other than fellow passen-gers. After about two hours, we returned to the plane. The blackout of the win-dows wasn't lifted until the plane was well on its way.

Our best guess was that we had stopped at a U.S. Military facility on one of the Aleutian Islands, probably pretty close to the Siberian peninsula of Kam-chatka. My doctor friend Ed said the island was Shemya. It was easy to under-stand why the U.S. had developed such facilities when you looked at the map. Japan had been a hostile military power for years, and so had the Soviet Union. The Aleutian Islands were strategically located for our defense (or offense) against both. On the map, the chain of islands looked like a curved sword aimed at the heart of Asia. There was no telling what awesome firepower we had hidden underground on those islands.

Anxiety built up in me as we approached Japan. I had so many questions on what it was going to be like that only time could answer. I was physically, mentally, and emotionally exhausted after three eight-hour flights with two weird stops. But there it was before me: Japan, "The Land of the Rising Sun." WOW!

The passengers gave an appreciative round of applause when the landing gear touched down. A U.S. Army sergeant boarded the plane and asked the U.S. Military personnel to wait until the civilian passengers had deplaned, then to follow him. He led us to a bus and said he would be taking us to Camp Drake on the outskirts of Tokyo just as soon as our footlockers and duffle bags were loaded. The drive from Haneda Airport was picturesque and thrilling. Everything appeared to be in miniature and seemed different and quaint—the architecture, the vehicles, the people and the way they were dressed, even the strange-looking vegetation. As we entered Tokyo, the traffic (they drive on the left) became more congested. When we stopped at a red light I had a real cultural shock. I noticed people urinating right out there in public—the men against walls or trees, the women squatting, spreading their skirts around them and getting that contented look on their face. My doctor friends just shrugged. What could you say? Then I noticed people wearing white gauze masks over their nose and mouth area. Ed explained that it was Japanese custom when one had a cold. Many of the women had infants on their backs—papoose style—with the kids' heads wobbling around and the poor little things trying to hold on for dear life. Again, Ed maintained there was no harm for the infant; the fact that the infant was forced to use its hands at that age developed its small motor movements. Most men, as well as women and children, were wearing traditional Japanese clothing—kimonos of one style or another. The men who were wearing Western-style business suits seemed out of place.

Camp Drake had been a Japanese military facility during World War II, one of the many that General MacArthur had taken over for our purposes during the occupation. The accommodations were reasonably comfortable and featured a great Officer's Club with above average food service. The energetic and efficient Japanese waitresses were a pleasure. Instead of walking, they moved with a sort of hustling shuffle and a desire to please. What amazed me was how we managed the language barrier—lots of sign language and fast learning of simple words. Nevertheless, their English was far better than my Japanese. Two incidents stand out in my mind. The first relates to the extremely soft water—the kind that smells like rotten eggs. While showering, my wedding band slipped off my finger, bounced and rolled into the floor drain. Frustration doesn't begin to describe the experience of getting a Japanese plumber to retrieve my ring. One of the problems was that the hot water valve was on the right rather than on the left. The second incident occurred at breakfast on the morning of March 5—the traumatic news that the Soviet dictator, Joseph Stalin, had died. The reaction was "good riddance." Otherwise, the routine was the same as the routine at Fort Lewis: check the bulletin board every morning, and then have the benefit of free time until the next morning. Somehow I felt tremendous relief. Whew! Apparently, I was not needed as a forward observer.

At our first opportunity, my two favorite doctors—Don and Ed—and I took a taxi into downtown Tokyo. First we went to the Tokyo On-Son, the famous bathhouse. This was a "must," according to Ed. The way he described it, we were in for a sensual experience. The facility was divided into lower class and higher class sections. Being U.S. Army officers, we qualified for higher class. In the lower class, men, women and children soaped themselves and rinsed off, standing on the ceramic tile deck surrounding the pool, then they got into the huge community pool that was filled with circulating hot spring water, and carried on conversations while they soaked themselves. The higher class area provided the privacy of your own bath and massage room, with two female attendants dressed in shorts and a halter. They undressed me, soaped me down, rinsed me off and guided me into a recessed tub filled with hot water to soak for a while. But Ed was wrong about the sensual experience. The attendants were highly professional, completely ethical (they handed me a wash rag for the private parts), and void of any sexuality. At one point during the massage, one of the attendants stood up on my back. She knew just how to step on the right pressure points to get the desired results. The bath, massage, manicure and pedicure left each of us feeling like a dishrag and ready for a drink or two.

As fast as we could, we headed to the Imperial Hotel on the Ginza, Tokyo's main street. The hotel was famous for having been designed by Frank Lloyd Wright, who devised some sort of springs in its foundation as earthquake protection. We designated its cocktail lounge as our official meeting place. After a couple of beers and gazing at Japanese TV, Don and Ed urged me go with them to see Kabuki at the Ernie Pyle Theater. Kabuki was a theatrical art form, dating back to the 1600s, where male actors played all of the characters—male, female, and even the horses. They wore elaborate costumes and heavy makeup. The plots centered on tragedy and sorrow, accompanied by weird music. At least that is how Ed described it. I went with them as far as the box office, but I begged off when I found out it was all in Japanese and lasted three hours. Ernie Pyle was an American war correspondent who was awarded the Pulitzer Prize for journalism for his coverage during World War II. He was killed by Japanese machine gun fire shortly before we dropped the atomic bomb on Hiroshima. I do not know who named the Kabuki Theater in his memory, but I can guess.

I headed back to the Ginza—the main street—and began my shopping tour at the Dai Itchy Building—the building General MacArthur selected as headquarters of the Far East Command. *(Dai Itchy* means "Number One.") There was a mystique about MacArthur. It was generally agreed that he could "walk on water", and he knew how to play the part. The building had an imposing location right across from the Imperial Palace grounds, with MacArthur's top-floor office looking down upon the palace. I would have loved to have seen the inside lobby, but white-helmeted, pristine looking MP's with chrome-plated rifles guarded the entrance, and I had no orders permitting me to enter, so I proceeded down the Ginza, meandering in and out of shopping arcades and interesting-looking places. When I entered a shop, someone would approach me, bow respectfully, hiss and try his best to please me. I wanted gifts for each member of our families and those ivory figurines for Dr. Weinstein. I did okay and got a few gifts sent, but I couldn't get my whole list completed in time to meet Don and Ed. My hope was that I would have at least one more opportunity to spend time in Tokyo.

Figure 2—THP on the Ginza across from the Imperial Palace

By the time I got back to the hotel, Ed had already been to the concierge and had made reservations for the three of us at an exclusive dinner club. This was a "Members Only" club, but they allowed commissioned officers of the U.S. Military. This particular club was more European or American in ambiance, rather than traditional Japanese. In this club the waiters wore tuxedoes, the hostesses wore satin evening gowns rather than Geisha kimono and obi, and the live orchestra played popular American music. Upon entering the club, each of us was assigned a hostess. The other patrons all appeared to be successful Japanese businessmen with their regular hostesses. (Wives never accompanied their husbands to such after-work places.) Our hostesses spoke English fairly well, and like geishas, they were trained as conversationalists. I had all sorts of questions to ask about my experiences that day. I was eager to sit down with English-speaking Japanese who were capable and willing to respond to my questions with answers other than "Japanese Custom," like I encountered in the shops. For instance, I thought I understood the custom of bowing—maybe not all of the repetitive bowing I witnessed—but what was all the hissing about? My hostess explained it this way: "In Japan, the higher the class (pronounced "crass"), the more hiss. The higher the class, the more respect. The more respect, the more bow." (The Japanese don't have the "L" sound in their language and pronounce "L" like "R." So, I became Rhutenant Parhet.) Okay, but I had lots of trouble understanding the class ranking system. After lots of questions and answers, I learned that class had a lot to do with bloodline, like in royalty. It also had to do with personal accomplishment. Japan was a fiercely competitive society. One had to be in the top percentage of his academic class to qualify for the next level of education: from middle school to high school to college, from college to graduate school, and so on, throughout life. Being a patriarchy-oriented society, we were talking almost exclusively about males. In old Japan, it was the samurai who were the highest caste. "But in modern Japan," my hostess explained, "the scholars and professors, master craftsmen and artists, authors and top performers, successful businessmen and politicians all garner higher and higher class levels as their careers and reputations ascend"—at least that's how I understood it. The roles of females in their society were quite different—mostly to please the males—to be good obedient wives, homemakers and mothers. This explained why men got on and off the elevators before the women and why women bowed first and avoided turning their backs to the men. The children, of course, were extremely well-disciplined and showed a remarkable, although a somewhat fearful respect for the father.

Our hostesses ordered our drinks the moment we sat down and never let a glass get near empty without ordering another. They interpreted the menu and ordered for us at exactly the right time so we would be served before the floor show. Right after they ordered, Ed got up to look for the men's room. His hostess understood. She popped up and led him away. When they returned, he looked at Don and me and said, "Gentlemen. are you in for an experience!"

When I decided to "go," I found out what he was talking about. My hostess led me to the restroom. It was mixed-sex. We entered together. There were urinals for the men and Eastern style commodes (recessed into the floor) for the females. It was a major shock to see everybody doing their business and going in and out together. The hostesses would help by turning on the water to wash your hands and handing you a towel to dry them on, and then lead you back to the table.

That experience was nothing, compared to the floor show. The first few acts were mostly vocalists singing Japanese songs (the #1 most popular song in Japan was "China Night") and popular American songs like "Black Magic," "I've Got You Under My Skin," "Oklahoma!" or "Blue Moon." They imitated the original artists so well, if you closed your eyes you thought Frank Sinatra, Dinah Shore or Johnny Mathis were up there singing. Then, after a Japanese dance act, the drums began to roll. Out came a Japanese youth, escorted by two scantily dressed young women. (It was difficult for me to tell their ages—about twenty, I'd guess.) The youth stood beside a platform while the young women undressed him. They eased him onto the platform, face up. Then, in a very ceremonial (sensual) way they got him aroused. He was huge. After more drums and fanfare, a wicker basket appeared above stage. In the basket was an extremely attractive young woman. The basket was specifically designed to hold the young woman's legs in a split position with her bottom exposed. Whoever was controlling the basket was really good. The basket—choreographed with the music—descended onto the youth. The action then became very graphic. When the act reached its climax, the audience politely applauded. That act in any night club in America, much less the university auditorium in Tuscaloosa, Alabama, would have "brought the house down," but the Japanese are such a reserved people they seem incapable of opening up and showing their unbridled emotions.

The next morning, hangovers were not bad enough; Don and Ed saw their names on the list. They had been assigned to an Eighth Army MASH Unit (Mobile Army Surgical Hospital), located somewhere within the Korean combat zone. I wished them well, told them I hoped to see them again, but not as a patient. Then I returned to my quarters to write a long letter to Louise while so many unusually interesting events were fresh on my mind.

Since my name did not appear on the assignment list day after day, I took advantage of the opportunities to visit Tokyo a few more times and enjoyed exploring and observing the strange culture. Why, I wondered, were the Japanese I met there so very different—except for their terrible-looking teeth—than the Japanese as portrayed to me when I was growing up? The Japanese I met in Japan were extremely polite, obviously intelligent, and industrious. Everything was very clean and orderly. I had expected them to be smaller than Americans, but I was still surprised at how short they really were. I felt so self-conscious in elevators and places like that, but I was truly puzzled at the differences from my preconceived image. My own conclusion centered on the power of wartime propaganda.

I was eleven years old when the Japanese attacked Pearl Harbor. For years before that, the Japanese had waged an aggressive war against the Chinese on the mainland. In school we learned that back in 1904 they fought with Russia over some frozen island, and the Japanese won. Then in 1910, their military seized and occupied Chosun, the Korean peninsula, and ruled it with a harsh, iron hand until it was liberated at the end of World War II. While growing up in New Orleans, my neighborhood friends, Joe Pasalaka, Hugh and Donald Vilavaso, Joey Krebs and I played "war" with toy soldiers and collected war cards, as well as baseball cards. The cards were included in bubble gum packages. Our mothers would take us to the "Five and Dime" store—Woolworth's or Kress's—for us to pick out the toy soldiers, tanks or cannons we needed. We played along the side yard of our home on Roman Street (4221). It was a perfect place to play, because nobody used it for anything else and we could leave all of our soldiers and fortifications there undisturbed until the next time we got the notion to play; it was the same for cowboys and Indians. The Germans, the Japanese and the Indians were the enemies. The Japanese were always portrayed as villainous, sinister, buck-toothed, squinty-eyed, bloodthirsty, ill-tempered little monsters, and the cards always showed them committing atrocities. They were portrayed similarly in the newspapers, magazines and newsreels that were shown at the movies. It was even worse in the featured movies about the war in the Pacific, where they were constantly referred to as "Japs." Actually, I hardly remember ever meeting, much less carrying on a conversation with a real live Japanese person before I was in Japan. My preconceptions were in sharp contrast with my personal experiences, and it was puzzling to me. I felt like I had been manipulated.

One particular discussion with a well-educated Japanese person helped me understand the Japanese mentality a little better. Japan, he explained, was a group of very mountainous islands, densely populated with no raw materials. Everything had to be imported. Japan wanted to stay independent and not become a colony of any other nation. The Dutch had captured and ruled Indonesia. The French ruled Southeast Asia—Vietnam, Laos and Cambodia—as well as some islands in the South Pacific Ocean. The Portuguese ruled Macao on the coast of China. The British ruled India, Burma, Hong Kong, and other parts of China. Japan feared that the Russians were going to come down on them from the North because the Russians needed a warm water port. The United States ruled the Philippines, Guam, Hawaii, the Aleutians and many other islands on their east. Japan felt surrounded by aggressive imperialist powers that wanted to extend their rule over them. So the Japanese people listened to their leaders, who convinced them they had to give their all in order to "Save Japan."

◆　　　◆　　　◆

My name finally appeared on the morning assignment list. I was designated as a "troop train commander" and was ordered to report to the Army's Transportation Office for instructions. The Major in charge told me I had been held up at Camp Drake until my security clearance came through. The clearance was required for my next assignment. He said the train was going to leave for Kure later that day. Kure was a mid-sized city on the Northern coast of the Inland Sea, located several hundred miles south of Tokyo. I was to be the commander of the two passenger cars—one for enlisted men and one for Officers—that the Army arranged to transport us, and he briefed me as to my duties. At Kure we would take a ferry to Eta Jima, one of the thousand or so islands in the Inland Sea. I, along with the others on the train, was to attend one of the several courses being taught there. My assignment was to attend the Chemical, Biological, and Radiological Warfare School in order to become CBR qualified. I needed the security clearance because of the classified material taught during the course.

The train ride was uneventful except for the excitement of passing Mt. Fuji. The Japanese countryside consisted of mostly villages surrounded by rice paddies, and what I could see of the towns was rather boring. The mountains, with lots of tunnels, sort of reminded me of driving on the turnpike through western Pennsylvania. These mountains, however, had rice paddies terraced up their slopes. Wherever you looked, there were rice paddies. Fortunately, my job as Troop Train Commander didn't amount to more than checking off names when we boarded the train and again when we got off. It was nighttime when we arrived, but I saw enough to whet my appetite for sightseeing and exploring—assuming I would get the opportunity.

Prior to the Japanese surrender that ended World War II, Eta Jima ("jima" means "island") was the "Annapolis"—the naval academy—of Japan. The campus was rather attractive and the setting was unusually beautiful. It overlooked the surrounding sea, with neighboring islands and serene Japanese gardens appearing here and there. Things were more Spartan inside the buildings, however. The officers' accommodations were barely adequate, as were the classroom buildings. The island was very hilly, and there was a picturesque fishing village within walking distance. The daily routine began with reveille, followed by the daily dozen. The classroom work took up three or four hours, and then there was a series of required lectures. These lectures were designed to qualify us to lecture others on the dangers of things like venereal disease, illegal drug use, hemorrhagic fever, and eating indigenous food or drinking the water. Otherwise, the rest of the time was free.

Figure 3—THP at CBR Warfare School, Eta Jima

We officers had a speedboat at our disposal. Mostly, it acted as a shuttle back and forth to Kure, which was close by. On weekends we could go to Hiroshima, which took much longer. Kure was the headquarters of the Australian Army's Korean Forces. I went to Kure one time. That was enough. The town was crawling with drunken Australian soldiers on R & R (Rest and Relaxation) from the combat zone. Most had a Japanese prostitute on their arm. They were unbearably loud and vulgar, and every sentence they yelled out had to include "bloody c**t" in it. The little town on Eta Jima wasn't much better. When we went into town to walk around and explore, beggars, vendors and young boys soliciting sex for their sisters constantly pestered us. I found it much more comfortable just hanging around the campus, spending time in the officers' club, writing letters and taking pictures. I had purchased a Japanese-made 35-millimeter camera in Tokyo and was learning how to use it.

The CBR Warfare course was extremely interesting. Special emphasis was placed on the biological warfare segment. At the time, the Communist Chinese government was openly accusing the United States of waging Germ Warfare against them on the Chinese mainland. The fear on our part was that China would use that allegation to justify retaliation by using biological agents against our troops in Korea. Officially, the United States emphatically denied the allegation. Our instructor assured us that we were definitely not using any biological agents against them. He admitted, however, that we were dropping propaganda leaflets over the mainland from extremely high-flying planes. Mao Tse Tung was using the highly publicized allegations to motivate the population to clean up their cities and to practice better hygiene. Regardless, the school intensified its efforts to prepare us for the possibility that biological agents would be used.

The highlight of the chemical warfare course was going into a gas chamber. We entered the chamber, wearing protective suits and gas masks. They also put some caged mice in there with us. In order to bolster our confidence, they released different types of gas to prove to us that the equipment worked. The mice dropped dead. The climax was when they had us take off our masks in order to experience the affects of tear gas. Strong stuff!

My favorite subject was radiological warfare. It was highly informative. It included the whole body of knowledge that had been learned from the first successful test of an Atomic Bomb in the desert of Nevada to the dropping of the bombs on Hiroshima and Nagasaki. Our instructor took us to Hiroshima for on-sight instruction and observations—fascinating, awesome and frightening. It had been eight years since the blast. He showed us silhouettes of men, women, and children—some riding bicycles—that were burned into the concrete bridges and granite steps of sturdily built bank and government buildings. He took us to the ruins of the reinforced concrete building they calculated as being at ground zero directly below the explosion. Despite the awesome blast and the intense heat, some of the masonry walls were still standing and there were mangled steel beams that had supported the dome, but the rest was mostly debris. Surviving victims, scarred and maimed, were ever present. Many were begging. They had enormous success with us.

Graduation took place in the main auditorium. It included the receiving of a certificate, orders for our next assignment, and listening to a speech. My orders specified that I report to the QMC-KCOMZ (Korean Communication Zone) Headquarters in Pusan, Korea, for further assignment. A colonel who had just returned from a year in Korea delivered the speech. I was impressed with the advice he gave us on how to deal with Asians. "You do not come on direct or strong," he emphasized. "You patiently engage in small talk and social niceties until you have cultivated a pleasant relationship and a feeling of mutual confidence." He related some personal anecdotes and told a couple of jokes in order to explain the Asian mentality and sense of humor. The first joke had to do with some American Flying Tigers during World War II who were flying a cargo plane cram full of Chinese coolies (laborers) to help build the Burmese Highway. While passing over the Himalayan Mountains, the crew heard riotous laughter coming from the rear. The co-pilot opened the door to the cargo section, found a coolie who spoke English, and asked him what all the commotion was about. The coolie explained, "Door open—coolie fall out plane."

"What's so funny about that?" asked the co-pilot.

"He no have parachute!" laughed the coolie.

The second joke had to do with a Korean family who had fled Seoul when the North Korean Army invaded at the beginning of the war. This family, like thousands of others, grabbed what possessions they could carry and headed south toward Pusan in front of the invaders. An American officer with the U.S. 24th Infantry Division happened to notice that the papa-san was riding on his ox in the front, while walking behind him were the mama-san and the children, carrying loads on their heads and backs. The officer asked the papa-san about this seemingly unfair arrangement. The papa-san responded, "Korean custom."

United Nations forces were able to stop the invaders around the Pusan Perimeter, pull off the Inchon invasion, cut off and surround the North Koreans, putting them in disarray and in retreat. When the refugees down in Pusan felt secure, they packed up again and headed north. The same American officer happened to see the same Korean family heading back to Seoul, but now the mama-san and the children were walking up front and the papa-san was riding on his ox at the rear. So, the officer asked the papa-san why the difference? Papa-san answered, "Landmines."

The next morning we graduates went by ferry to Hiroshima, and then by train across the island to Sasebo, which is located directly across the Sea of Japan from Pusan. Sasebo was teaming with military personnel from various United Nations' forces going to and coming from Korea. The harbor was loaded with war ships of all descriptions. The whole scene was exciting, like a bustling war movie set.

My main thought? The fun was over. Now I was on my way to join the war…

Figure 4—THP leaving Sasebo. The sign on the building reads:
"Through this port pass the best damn fighting men in the world."

3

Introducing: Korea

A seven-piece, uniformed Japanese band was on the pier playing marching music as we climbed up the wobbly gangway to board the troop ship. The ship had been hastily built during World War ll and was very tired. All it did was ferry troops back and forth from Sasebo to Pusan. When we applauded, the conductor turned around and bowed repeatedly, then led the band in "Anchor's Away" as the ship pulled away from the pier. The trip to Pusan lasted all night in stormy seas. I had motion sickness the entire time. I never thought I'd be thankful to get to Korea. As if I wasn't sick enough, the place was crowded, drab and filthy. Army trucks took us to our assignments. The roads were filled with potholes and the air stunk.

The QMC personnel replacement headquarters was located in Tanggok, a suburb east of Pusan. It was on the road to K-9, the U.S. Air Force airport for Pusan—directly across the road from the entrance to the United Nations Military Cemetery (UNMC). The clerk on duty at the HQ first sent me to the bursar to exchange my greenbacks for Military Script. (It was a court-marshal offense for U.S. Military personnel to possess greenbacks while in Korea. It was the army's way of fighting the black market). Then the clerk told me where to find my bunk and the bulletin board, where every morning I was to look for my name on the assignment list. If my name wasn't on the list, I was free for the rest of the day. I took a badly needed hot shower and a nap. Feeling refreshed, I went to the Officers' Club. I talked with a few of the officers who were just sitting around. They told me it was a major hassle to go into Pusan. The city had 85,000 before the war; now there were three million. Exiles from the North were all over the place, especially around the train and bus stations—in every nook and cranny. Each day some died from exposure, disease, or malnutrition and a truck went around picking them up. Filthy kids with runny noses and covered with sores were begging, trying to pick your pockets or cutting the shoulder strap of your camera and running off with it. Nearby, the only place of any interest was the cemetery. That was the last place I wanted to go.

I spent a lot of time trying to reach Gus Freibaum by using the primitive telephone system, and I finally succeeded. Gus was a year ahead of me at 'BAMA. He was the president of **ZBT** Fraternity in his senior year; I was vice-president. He had been in Korea a year and was ready to return stateside. We had been corresponding and he filled me in on his experiences. He had been assigned to the QM Supply Depot in Pusan. The depot was near the harbor. All of the quartermaster supplies for all U.S. Forces in Korea were sent there from the States by freighters. The supplies were unloaded by hundreds of Korean stevedores, warehoused, and then sent out as needed in trucks and by railroad. Gus and another fraternity brother, Julian Kayser, somehow got the use of a jeep. They came by and picked me up and took me to the depot for dinner. This depot was responsible to supply the 350,000 or so American forces in Korea at the time. I had never seen a facility that huge. Warehouses stretched as far as the eye could see. Trucks, forklifts and workers were bustling with activity. The commanding general and the usual field grade officers and between 300 and 400 QM Lieutenants—mostly ROTC graduates—ran the operation along with thousands of non-commissioned officers, enlisted men, and Korean civilians.

We had dinner at the "Bama" table. In addition to Gus and Julian, Jessie Weatherly, Sam Christopher, Barry Ackman, Alan Barton and several others I cannot recall were there. I really enjoyed being with them and hearing all about life at the QM Supply Depot and catching up on all the news. It seemed like they knew everything going on with everybody. Barry had just heard that his girl friend, Anne Silberman, had been accepted into a very high level position in Washington, DC and that's all he talked about. Anne was from Birmingham. She was a close friend and sorority (AEPhi) sister of Louise at 'Bama'. It just seemed certain that I would end up at the QM Supply Depot.

◆   ◆   ◆

"Lt. Pailet, we have reviewed your file and are convinced you are the right officer to replace Lt. Edwards, who is set to rotate stateside," said the friendly personnel officer. "You will join the 114th Graves Registration Company. This company is under United Nations command rather than U.S because it provides services to all the participating forces. The UN command HQ is in Teague." The blood drained from my face. He must have noticed, because he assured me that this was a choice assignment. It would be rewarding as well as challenging.

"While you are getting your gear, I'll get a jeep to take you to the company's headquarters. It is right across the road."

The Quartermaster Corps provided a wide array of services necessary to nourish and support the combat units. Among other things, it provided the food, clothing, petroleum products and a variety of necessary supplies and services. In the combat zone it operated mobile kitchens, bakeries, laundries, shoe repair and supply units that were designed to keep up with the moving armies. Back at Fort Lee, VA, in the Officers' Training Course, they taught us how to operate and command all of the different QMC units, even parachute maintenance and repair—everything except Graves Registration. That is the service of dealing with the deceased. All I remembered was a casual mention, "Oh, we are also responsible for Graves Registration. The work is very specialized. In the unlikely event any of you are assigned to one of those units they will train you, so we won't spend time on that."

Captain Welsh, the company commander, was a tall man in his middle 30s with a balding pate. He had a gaunt look with dark circles around his eyes and a cigarette dangling out of his mouth. He earned his commission during World War II and stayed in the reserves after the war. In his civilian life he had sold men's clothes. He seemed like a likable guy. He gave me a warm welcome and explained that Lt. Edwards was on his way from Sach'on. He didn't expect him to arrive until dinnertime because Edwards didn't leave until he received word that his replacement had been selected.

The 114th's search and recovery platoon was stationed in Sach'on. Its mission was to search the Pusan Perimeter for missing-in-actions. Sach'on was about 80 miles west of Pusan, but the road was so bad it took about six hours by jeep. "C'mon, Lieutenant," said the captain, "let me show you around the compound while we have the time."

The place was much more extensive than I had imagined—more than 72 acres. The headquarters compound occupied a 15-acre site and it was surrounded by a chain-link and barbed wire security fence. There were eight quonset huts of various sizes, a mess hall large enough to feed this company at full strength—about 150 men, and a motor pool. There were separate huts for administration, living quarters for commissioned officers, for non-commissioned officers, UN liaison personnel, three for the enlisted men and one latrine. The grounds were immaculate, with little white picket fences around the flower gardens. As we toured, everybody (reluctantly) snapped to attention and saluted. Welsh introduced me to every person we encountered, including his personal interpreter; Captain Yon of the ROK (Republic of Korea) Army. Somehow I sensed that they all feared Welsh. An orphanage with loads of children with high-pitched voices was on the other side of the fence near the motor pool. Welsh took great pride in telling me that the 114th had an ongoing program to help the orphans.

Figure 5—114th QM HQ compound

Adjacent to the headquarters compound was the Operations compound. Within its secured area were the mortuary, its administrative offices, a chapel and access to the internment areas. Welsh showed me the administration quonset first. It included his private office, desks for four clerk-typists, a radio room, and a lot of file cabinets. On the way to the mortuary quonset we passed about 60 black body bags stacked up like cord wood and filled with recently deceased. I was struck by a strong odor that I could not identify. Welsh explained that the bodies had just arrived from the combat zone and were sprayed with wintergreen while they were waiting to be processed. Reluctantly, I followed him into the mortuary. There it smelled like formaldehyde, which was used in the embalming process. He showed me the small outer office and then the working area. It was lined with examining tables—ten on each side of the center isle. Each contained a corpse in a different state of mutilation, with a mortician attending to it. Welsh introduced me to each mortician. Then he explained the entire processing procedure: identification, inventory of and securing of the personal effects, the embalming and disposition (internment here or transport to home country). I had never before seen a dead body. I tried my best to keep my composure. I felt like throwing up. Welsh sensed my discomfort. As we left, he said, "At first, it was very difficult for me to even enter that room, but after a short time I found myself walking through the mortuary while eating an ice cream cone and thinking nothing of it."

I asked myself, "Is it possible I could ever get hardened to what I just witnessed?" I thought for a moment, and then I replied, "Captain, all I can hope is that I will become comfortable in there without becoming calloused."

From there we headed to the internment areas—first to the enemy cemetery. It stretched over several rolling hills toward the ocean. White grave markers lined up in perfectly straight rows. Welsh suspected, though, that in the early days of the war they just dumped bodies of the enemy into pits and covered them up. Then they put out the markers. From our vantage point the markers appeared to merge into the white-capped ocean. The deathly still white markers juxtaposed against the dancing white caps struck me. I asked, "How many enemy were buried there?"

Welch answered, "It is estimated that so far the NKPA (North Korean Peoples' Army) had lost at least 500,000 and the Chinese Communists around a million, but no one other than God Almighty knows for sure how many of them are buried here. C'mon, let's move on."

The United Nations section of the cemetery was aesthetically striking—very colorful. Flags of all the participating countries flew proudly. The UN flag was front-row-center between flags of the U.S. and the Republic of Korea. Others were: Australia, Belgium/Luxembourg, Canada, Colombia, Denmark, Ethiopia, France, Greece, India, Italy, Netherlands, Norway, New Zealand, Philippines, Republic of South Africa, Sweden, Thailand, Turkey, and the United Kingdom.

In addition to the name and nationality, the religion of the deceased was designated with appropriate markers: Crosses, Stars of David, or Crescent & Star—all painted stark white. There were facilities for ceremonies and a special monument to three unknown soldiers in front of the UN flag. That was where visiting dignitaries laid a wreath and had their picture taken. As we were leaving the area, Welsh said, "Oh, over there behind that stone wall is the non-belligerent section. We have some UN Observers—Poles and Swedes who were killed in vehicle accidents or by land mines. And we have six Russian Mig pilots that were shot down and fished out of the water by our Navy. We're just warehousing them until somebody tells me what to do with'em. Right now our State Department denies that we have any Russians because the Soviets deny any active participation in the fighting."

Figure 6—The UNMC from a hilltop

Figure 7—Enemy Cemetery

"C'mon, Pailet, you look like you could use a drink." Truer words have never been spoken.

The officers' quonset, called the BOQ (Bachelor Officers Quarters), had a very comfortable lounge area. Kim, a hard-working youth of about 16, was the houseboy. He did all of the cleaning, laundry, polishing and shining. He also tended bar in the lounge. That's where we were when Lieutenant Edwards drove up in his jeep. Welsh introduced us and questioned Edwards about the drive. He really got angry when Edwards told him he didn't bring a "shotgun" because he knew it would crowd things on the return trip. He didn't even wear his steel helmet. Welsh chewed him out big time. It made me feel terrible, as if he had risked his life because of me. Later, in private, he explained that after a couple of drinks

Welsh's personality changed like Dr. Jeckell and Mr. Hyde. Plus, he said, "It doesn't help matters with him that I am a Negro."

I had not heard the term "shotgun" since I was a kid. My friends and I went to the movies every Friday night. Most of the films were cowboy and Indian ones: Gene Autry, Roy Rogers, the Lone Ranger and all the other Wild West thrillers. Every horse-drawn stagecoach had a driver holding the reins with one hand and a whip in the other, lashing out at the galloping horses. Sitting next to the driver was the "shotgun"—the good guy with the rifle at ready looking out for the bad guys—the outlaws or the Indians.

Negro (colored or black) QMC officers were rare; the corps had not been racially integrated very long. Integrating the armed forces was one of the first things Eisenhower did when he became Commander-in-Chief. There was only one Negro in my class at Ft Lee. When he and his wife showed up at the officers' club swimming pool, it was the first time in my life I had seen black people in bathing suits. It was a cultural shock to me; the swimming pools and the beaches were strictly segregated in the South while I was growing up.

Edwards projected a clean, competent, military appearance. He had a "good face," a pleasant, deep speaking voice, and I liked him the moment we met. After cocktails we stopped at the latrine on our way to the mess hall—my first experience of being in a bathroom or, later, sitting at the same dinner table with a colored person.

What a day! When I got to my room and plopped down on my cot, I wrote to Louise and to my folks. I had not heard from home in almost six weeks. I finally had a mailing address, but I knew it would be at least two weeks before this letter would get there and another two weeks before a reply could catch up with me.

The next morning at breakfast, Welsh told me he had made arrangements for "my" S&R platoon to move from Sach'on Air Force Base to Masan. Edwards, he said, would fill me in on the details. Then they gave me a steel helmet, a 45-caliber pistol as my personal weapon and a 30-caliber carbine to ride shotgun. After Kim loaded the jeep and secured the cargo against theft, Edwards and I drove off.

It took quite awhile to drive through Pusan. There wasn't much vehicular traffic—a few UN jeeps or trucks, an occasional Korean bus or truck and a few slow moving ox-drawn carts. The only sedans were official government-owned. The people crowding the streets were oblivious to us. Most of the women had large loads balanced on their heads. Children were playing in the middle of the street. Occasionally a kid would come up to our jeep and touch it just to see what it felt like. Some of the women and children had infants strapped on their backs. Many of the men had A-frames on their backs loaded with all sorts of cargo—from "honey buckets" to furniture. White-clad Papa-sans with black stove pipe hats stopped to talk to each other with no regard as to where they were standing. It did little good to blow the horn. Edwards just had to maneuver his way through.

Papa-san, mama-san, professor-san—the suffix "san," I learned, was an expression of respect, a formal and honorable salutation or reference. When a Korean gentleman reached the age of retirement, he would begin wearing the traditional black hat, white cotton, full-length gown, tied with a tasseled belt and let his mustache and goatee grow. He and his peers would smoke those long, skinny, little-bowled pipes, and dispense wisdom to the young.

After we finally got out of the congestion of Pusan, we could relax somewhat and carry on a conversation. Edwards loved to talk. He explained that the S&R platoon had been quartered within the Korean Air Force training center in Sach'on for the past two years. From that base the platoon searched the Western edge of the Pusan Perimeter. Fierce combat occurred all along the Perimeter, which took place over a six-week period in late summer of 1950. That was where the U.S. Commander, General Walker, after consultation with MacArthur of course, gave the famous "stand or die" order. The United States and Republic of Korea armies made their stand at great cost, but they stopped the NKPA's (North Korean Peoples' Army) advance. There was a lot of back-and-forth fighting and a lot of hand-to-hand combat. One side would charge up a hill to take the high ground, and then the other side would counterattack. Not only were there lots of killed and wounded, but also this type of fighting created a lot of missing-in-actions (MIA's). Their sacrifice followed by the success of the Inchon Landing reversed the momentum of the war.

◆   ◆   ◆

Korea was remarkably undeveloped. It had few roads; the only ones paved were the main streets in the urban areas. In the south there were mostly hills and valleys and agricultural lands. There was one railroad running from Pusan through Teagu to Seoul, one halfway decent river, the Naktong, and few deep-water ports. North Korea had the minerals, the electro-power and the industry, and it had cut off the supply of electricity to the South. There was at least one village in each valley. The people were genuine peasants. They built their own little one-room thatched-roof homes out of handmade mud bricks smeared with clay. The floors were also dried clay, but they had an ingenious heating system. Outside a wall at one end of the structure was a small pot-belly stove. Mama-san would put a cake made out of crushed coal under the stovetop then light it so it smoldered. She would use the heat to cook the daily soup and rice, and in the winter she directed the smoke into clay pipes that had been laid under the floor. This would heat the floor and keep the home comfortably warm, regardless of how cold it got. Rice paddies were everywhere the farmers could put them and it was plowing time. The farmers were out there with their ox-drawn hand plows, just like they had been doing for the past thousand or so years. They spread human waste to fertilize their fields. The odor was awful—beyond description.

Figure 8—Honey Bucket

Figure 9—Honey Wagon

Driving those mountainous roads was scary; they were unpaved with narrow, hairpin turns, steep drops with no guardrails and little, if any, sight distance. These roads were not built for motorized vehicles; they were built for pedestrians, or at the most ox-drawn wagons. We had to share these "paths" with village mama-sans carrying huge loads on their heads. Some of them had exposed breasts in order to nurse the infants on their backs. When their babies got hungry, they would just swing the little one around to the front and go about their business. There was also the occasional farmer with a loaded A-frame or an ox cart, moving along like molasses in the winter time. The scariest of all was encountering a bus—old and dented—loaded beyond belief with peasants and their possessions strapped to the top. These busses always seemed to list to one side or the other. Our progress was measured, as the expression went, "in hours per mile, rather than miles per hour."

Many MIA files were yet to be searched in the area around Sach'on. According to Edwards, the decision to move the platoon to Masan was made because Sach'on was isolated from other U.S. facilities and there had been a noticeable increase in guerrilla activity in the area. Quite a few North Koreans were still trapped in South Korea. The Inchon Landing had cut them off. They took to the hills and were living off of the land—raiding and terrorizing villages, stealing their rice, chickens and pigs. Every day the ROK army sent patrols out, looking for the guerrilla hideouts. Edwards showed me warning signs posted along roads and in the towns, alerting the citizens to the danger. Oddly, some villagers were sympathetic to the Communist cause and secretly helped the guerrillas. During the invasion, of course, most villagers evacuated and headed for Pusan when the NKPA was advancing. On the other hand, there were those who stayed in their village and even gave comfort to the Communists. Then Edwards started telling me about the land mines. He did a good job of explaining all this to me, but it was difficult for me to concentrate. I was having a very difficult time realizing this was really me in this situation.

Masan was 50 miles from Pusan. It took almost four hours to get there because the road conditions were so bad. We entered the town, continued along the main road to town center, and then made a right turn. Edwards drove up a winding road to a plateau where the UN Headquarters compound was located. It was neat as a pin, in sharp contrast to what I had seen of this town. Masan was a port town. The UN located its salvage operations there. All of the salvageable articles of war—weapons, equipment, trucks, jeeps, helmets, combat boots, fatigues, canteens, even tanks—were sent here for disposition. There was an attempt to restore some of the items to reusable condition, but most were sorted out and dumped onto individual piles. Then each pile was auctioned off to scrap dealers who would come from all over the world, each in his own freighter, to bid on this stuff.

Edwards and I were caked with dust and grime, having traveled in an open jeep, so we stopped at the officer's latrine to wash up before he introduced me to the post commander, a full ('Bird') Colonel from Mobile, Alabama. He gave what seemed to me a reluctant welcome, showed me the area where the platoon would be quartered, my living quarters and the quonset that I would use as the platoon's operational headquarters. Then he led us to the Officer's Club to get something to eat. Above the main entrance was the sign, "Top of the Mark."

The ride to Sach'on was easier because the hills were not nearly as high and the road was better. However, there were several streams to cross. All of the bridges had been destroyed during the fighting. None had yet been rebuilt. When we came to a stream, Edwards had to stop the jeep, shift into four-wheel-drive, and ford the stream. Each time he would point out the best way to ford that particular stream to avoid getting mired down, despite the advantages of four-wheel-drive. Once he had me get out of the jeep and push from the rear, just in case. Otherwise, during this segment of the trip he concentrated on explaining the details of the platoon's operations. It was divided into four teams (squads). Each team consisted of a leader, four U.S. Army personnel (one of which operated the land mine detector), and four Korean laborers (at least one of which was capable of interpreting). My job was to assign MIA files to each team and review the files with the team leaders each morning before they left to conduct their search. My job was to also inspect the team's truck—all of its equipment and weapons to make sure everything was operational—then each day I was to have my driver take me out to check on the progress of the teams.

Sach'on was situated on the southern coast of Korea, about 8 miles south of Chinju, and was a charming little town overlooking a small bay. Cherry trees were everywhere, and it was cherry blossom time. Enchanting. The Korean Air Force Training Center was on the outskirts of town. We arrived in time for Edwards to show me around and take me to "our" area. It was located in a far corner of the Center against the barbed wire fence that "protected" the Center. There were five olive-green squad-sized tents—headquarters, plus one for each team. The platoon's trucks were parked next to the headquarters tent. My quarters—if you want to call them that—were located at the rear of the headquarters tent. They consisted of a cot and some shelves for my things. My cot was between the platoon's gun rack and the shelves. I was anxious about meeting the platoon.

"Where are the men?" I asked.

"They have already finished for the day. They are either at the mess hall or at their hootchies." Edwards answered, trying to hide his embarrassment.

"Their h-hootchies?" I asked in my innocent ignorance.

"You'll see the men in the morning. They spend the nights in town with their girlfriends." Edwards had a hard time getting that out. Then he said, "I'm gonna show you the officers' club, where you'll have your meals. Then I'm gonna take off 'til morning, Okay?"

"Okay," I answered in total shock.

Edwards turned to leave, then he stopped abruptly and turned back to me. He said, "Pailet, let me explain how lucky you are to have this assignment. You'll be your own boss. You can type out your own orders to go anywhere you want at any time, even Japan. Most times you won't even need written orders like every other officer in Korea; just show your GR (Graves Registration) insignia to the guard at the gate or the MP (military police) and tell 'em you're on official business. They'll never question you." His expression showed that he thought he had made me feel better. Then he turned around again and left.

◆   ◆   ◆

The Korean officers' club did its best to accommodate my taste. They had a supply of rations that had been provided by the mess sergeant in Masan, but the cooks didn't know what to do with them. Since Edwards didn't eat there, nobody cared, so I had to make do with some of the rations and some of the Korean food that I felt was safe to eat. But there were a great many questions swirling around in my head!

After dinner I found the way back to my tent, with some difficulty, because of the confusing layout, plus it was getting dark. While I was writing a letter to Louise, a security guard with a rifle in his hand banged on the entrance to my tent and demanded (in Korean) that I turn off my lantern. I obeyed, even though I didn't know why. Then I looked outside: total darkness. I had to grope my way around the tent. I got my pistol—the 45—out of its holster and a carbine off the gun rack, then I crawled into my cot. About an hour later I heard some rustling going on outside my tent. It sounded just like some guerillas were cutting the barbed wire fence with wire cutters. I held the 45 in my right hand and had the carbine where I could fire it. More rustling. Then I heard a ripping sound—the sound of somebody cutting the canvas on the side of my tent. Shivering with fright, I pulled the blanket over my head and cocked my 45. Would I freeze up? Would I be able to pull the trigger point blank, even at a guerilla? They said that a 45-caliber bullet tears a human being apart at close range. Cautiously, I peeked out of the covers; my eyes had adjusted somewhat to the dark. We were taught to use our peripheral rather than straight-ahead vision. Soon I figured out what it was. *Rats!* At least a dozen huge, ugly rats with shiny eyes and long tails. There was nothing I could do but pray they wouldn't jump on my bed, not be carrying the fleas that gave you hemorrhagic fever, and would leave before dawn. What a night!

Figure 10—THP at HQ tent—Sachon

The door of the tent swung open. "Good morning, Lieutenant; meet Sergeant O'Brien, your second in command," shouted Edwards. We shook hands, greeted each other, and while O'Brien was nervously explaining that the men were getting their things together for the move to Masan, Edwards interrupted. "Sergeant, I'm gonna take the lieutenant to the officers' mess for some breakfast while you get everything ready." At breakfast I tried to tell Edwards about last night.

He explained, "Oh, the guard did that because of 'Bed-Check-Charlie'. Sometimes on moonless nights the Commies fly a little single-engine plane over the base. They do it to terrorize. The pilot tries to cause some damage by dropping mortar shells and hand grenades out of the plane. He aims at anything he can see. We don't know where the plane comes from. If we ever sighted the little bastard we'd shoot'em down, but they pick the darkest nights. You'll have the same thing in Masan—even more so." I decided not to mention the rats.

◆   ◆   ◆

What a motley, incongruous looking caravan! I was embarrassed. U.S. Army trucks filled with a mixture of disheveled U.S. GI's, Korean laborers and a wide variety of indigenous (native) people with all their possessions—even some pets. Edwards and I were in the lead jeep, along with a small boy named Kim. Pfc. (private first class) Mike Casey was driving.

◆   ◆   ◆

The small boy, Kim Yung Min, was five years old when the NKPA invaded Seoul. He was separated from his family during the tumultuous confusion. He became a refugee, then headed south with the throngs of others. He had a limp. During a mortar attack a piece of shrapnel had lodged in his hip. Edwards' girl-friend had assumed the role of a foster parent—seeing to it that Kim was well cared for and attended school. He impressed me as being a bright, attractive nine-year-old—loaded with personality and intelligence and who spoke surprisingly good English.

Figure 11—Caravan from Sachon to Masan

Figure 12—Papa-sans

Edwards called a halt to the caravan just before it entered Masan. He took Kim with him, while he and Sgt. O'Brien went from truck to truck giving orders. They had a plan on how they would relocate their hootchies in Masan. Then Edwards drove the jeep up the hill to the "Top of the Mark." We reported in. Then he took my gear and me to my BOQ, informed me that he was taking Pfc. Casey with him, said his good-bye and his good luck, jumped into the jeep and headed for Pusan. The house girl ran out and carried my duffle and footlocker into my room. There was a 2nd lieutenant leaning against the door jam. "Hi, my name is Harry Martin. Welcome."

4

Search and Recovery

The weather was gloomy, cold and rainy. I got up and out early—the first one in the platoon HQ. I wanted to get my office and desk organized. During the night I don't think I got any sleep; I was excited. I kept thinking about what I was going to say and how I would handle myself. When Sgt. O'Brien finally came into the HQ quonset I said, "Sergeant, pull up a chair, there are some things we need to talk about." Among other things, I told him that when I reported in to the base commander he said, "Lieutenant, I realize you are not responsible for the reputation of your platoon, but now that you're quartered here with me you either get your outfit straightened out or else!" I told him that he said it in an ugly, threatening way. "He wasn't specific," I explained to O'Brien, "but I can guess what he meant. The men have a slovenly, unmilitary-like appearance and he probably knows about their off-base living conditions. I hope there isn't any-thing serious—like drugs." I asked O'Brien to level with me so we could get off to a good start. He assured me that there was nothing serious, that he would cor-rect the situation, and he promised immediate results. I told him that I wanted him to devote the day to this and that I wanted to become acquainted with the men, the equipment, and the MIA files.

Figure 13—Sgt. O'Brien

Figure 14—Pfc Casey

O'Brien had a tough assignment. These men had gone what was referred to as "native." They no longer resembled a military unit. While O'Brien was working on straightening out the platoon, I had him send each member of the platoon—one at a time—into my office for a private session. I had each man give me a brief personal history. Then I asked questions. The first one to come in was Pfc. Casey. He had been private driver and "gofer" for Lt. Edwards. Casey was very personable—a wheeler-dealer type with a gift of gab. He had grown up in Boston and had been drafted after high school graduation. When I told him I wanted him to continue as my driver, he thanked me profusely.

Other than Casey, two others made a favorable impression on me. The first was Pvt. Richard "Dick" Priest from Kingston, NY, also drafted. He was the platoon's clerk-typist and radio operator. The other was Corporal Ernest "Ernie"

Modarelli from Jersey City, one of the team leaders. Those three were very likable. The other men were non-descript—marking time until they could go home. Some were well educated. It seemed that any college-educated draftee who studied anything with "ology" after the name—like "physiology"—was assigned to Graves Registration. A few had graduate degrees. But there was a definite bitterness that came through—perhaps resentment of my disturbing their freedom. I tried to cultivate a relationship of mutual respect for our positions. I reviewed what I expected of them and what they could expect of me. I assured them that they could depend on weekend passes as long as they conformed to the rules of the base. Naturally, I realized there would be a lot of bitching. We were taught at Officers' Training School that as long as the troops were bitching, things were normal. It's when they *weren't* bitching that you had to worry.

Figure 15—Cpl Modarelli

The last to come in was Mr. Lee. He had been born and raised under Japanese occupation in the city of Pyongyang, the capitol of what had become The People's Republic of North Korea. When he was a teenager the Japanese forcibly took him from his family and sent him to Japan to work on their railroad system. He lived there until he was able to return to Korea after the Japanese surrender in 1945. Mr. Lee was a pleasant, 40-odd year old man, rather shy and subservient, and he bowed a lot just like the Japanese. His clothes were clean, but wrinkled—a white, cotton tee shirt (despite the cold, damp weather), black, baggy pants and those ubiquitous rubber shoes, which I had been noticing on most Koreans. His English was difficult for me to follow. Unfortunately for me, he reeked of that strong, distinctive odor which emanated from all of the Koreans with whom I'd been in close contact. I wasn't thrilled about having to spend a lot of time in close company with him.

Another thing that struck me was the frequent use of the expression, "no sweat." It seemed like "no sweat" was the response to almost every request of mine. It was used instead of "Yes," "OK," "All right," "I'll do it,"—an all-inclusive affirmative response. Instead of "Yes, sir," it was, "No sweat, Lieutenant (or Rutenant)," or just plain "No sweat."

The opposite of "no sweat" was "no way, GI."

◆   ◆   ◆

Thank goodness for Harry Martin. He and I had a great deal in common; we were the same age, both Jewish (the only ones within a 50 mile radius as far as we knew), both QM ROTC 2nd Lieutenants and living in the same quonset. He was engaged to Barbara. I, of course, was married to Louise. There were some notable differences. He grew up in the predominately Jewish neighborhood of Squirrel Hill in Pittsburgh. His religious orientation was traditional and his politics were Liberal. I grew up in predominately Catholic New Orleans. Even though I had become Bar Mitzvah at my family's traditional synagogue, I gravitated toward and embraced Reform, and my politics were Conservative—at least compared to Harry's. His room was directly across the hall from mine at the very rear of the quonset. Our house girl was Suzie—not her real name, but that's what we called her. Harry was assigned to the Korean Military Advisory Group (KMAG), which meant he was an advisor to the ROK Quartermaster Training School. He had his own jeep and his private interpreter—Captain Hain Paik Lee—who was a graduate of the University of Seoul. Capt. Lee was a good-looking fellow who spoke surprisingly good English. Harry gave me a tour of the facilities, and then we headed to the *Top of the Mark*. Compared to the food service I'd had since arriving in Korea, the cocktails and meals there seemed to me as if I was at the real "Top of the Mark" in San Francisco.

◆   ◆   ◆

O'Brien worked wonders with the men. It helped that their living conditions were improved. Now I was proud of my platoon. They looked good, their morale was up, and they took their work seriously. Every morning O'Brien and I met with each team leader. We had to know exactly where they would be that day. The U.S. Corps of Engineers kept us well-supplied with excellent topographical maps—the same quality as those used during our map-reading course at Ft. Lee. We would review the file or files of the particular MIA(s) that the team was to focus its search on. From the files we learned the nature of the fighting and could tell where the MIA (Missing in Action) had been when he was last seen or when his name last appeared on the morning report. It was important to know as much as possible. Every clue, regardless of how seemingly insignificant it was, could be crucial in making a recovery. After the briefing session, one of us would go out with the team leader and inspect the GI's, the laborers, the supplies and equipment, and set an expected time of return—usually an hour before sunset.

Figure 16—Search & Recovery Team

I experienced a rush of anxiety when Pvt. Priest said, "Lieutenant, here is a whole packet of mail for you." I took the packet to my room, closed the door and savored each and every word of every letter. It had been such a long time! My prayers were answered; everybody was well. It wasn't one of my prayers, but Louise had a job. She was a sportswear buyer at Gus Mayer, a ladies' clothing store on Church Street, the main shopping street in Nashville. I heard from her mother and father. They had been reading my letters with interest, but still wondered why the U.S. was involved in this ridiculous war 10,000 miles across the Pacific Ocean. My mother's letters weren't terribly newsy, but they were upbeat and loving. My brother Lester, whom I renamed "Brother" when he was born and I was four years old, told me he was counting the days until he would finish his freshman year at Tulane and start at the Parsons Institute of Art in New York City. All he really wanted to do was to doodle in class, but I had been urging him to leave Tulane with a good record, so he had begun to apply himself. He had a wonderful artistic talent and sense of design. I received a letter from Louise's grandmother Tuts and one from my Uncle Abie. He had served in the Pacific during World War II as a private in the infantry and was one of those who "hit-the-beach" at Okinawa. ("Brother" and I got a Cocker Spaniel and named him "Okie.") Joe Bernstein brought me up-to-date on what had been happening at Ft. Monmouth since I had left. He already knew whom, amongst our fraternity brothers (ZBT's from Alabama or Tulane) were in Korea: Gus Freibaum, Julian Kayser, "Spider" Klotzman, Barry Ackman and Alan Barton at the QM Depot in Pusan, and that Mark Golden was a lieutenant assigned to the 1st Marine Division. Receiving those letters was better than any tonic ever invented.

◆   ◆   ◆

I found Search & Recovery work to be enormously interesting. Every day was an adventure. I enjoyed going out into the Korean countryside to observe the teams at work, as well as the village life of the agrarian Koreans. The teams tried to recreate what was happening when the MIA was last seen. They did this while the mine detector was scanning the areas they needed to search. Pfc. Casey was such a character that it made the drives much more fun. Kim, the young little boy who had come to Masan with our caravan, began showing up in the mornings. He started pleading with me to take him along. Actually, he was a better interpreter than Mr. Lee, so one day when Mr. Lee couldn't go with me I agreed to let Kim come along. Afterwards, I tended to use Kim more and let Mr. Lee go out with O'Brien.

Figure 17—THP and Mr. Lee at a recovery site

One of the many things I found interesting was observing the school children. They all wore uniforms—each school had its distinctive look, but the uniforms were basically black. I would wave as I drove pass them, led by their teacher, walking single-file along the side of the road, and they would wave back. In the more remote areas, the kids rarely saw a motorized vehicle. Jeeps and trucks fascinated them. Occasionally, the boys would throw some of their things (pencils, books, rulers) in front of my jeep just to see the effect. After the jeep rolled over, for example a ruler, the kids would go pick up the pieces and "ooh" and "ah" at the damage.

◆　　　◆　　　◆

The post commander—that unpleasant "bird" colonel from Mobile, Alabama—summoned me to his office. First he warned me, "Never again do I want to hear about your men leaving human skulls on the hoods of your trucks. Never again! Do you understand me?" Next he handed me written orders, designating me as pre-trial defense counsel for the Masan area. I was already CBR warfare officer. Those orders came from the United Nations HQ in Teagu. The 114th Graves Registration Company was under that command because it provided services to all of the UN Forces. I think the colonel was antagonistic toward my platoon and toward me because I was not under his control. For example, he couldn't require that I take my turn as "Officer-of-the-Day" like all the other junior officers did. Harry Martin was the only other officer he couldn't control because of his KMAG status.

◆　　　◆　　　◆

Dick Priest was visibly upset. His earphones were still on. He shouted, "Lieutenant! Number Two Team blew two tires and is stranded at a Korean Police station near L'Chon Village."

I shouted back, "Go find Sergeant O'Brien and Mr. Lee." I got Pfc. Casey to load my jeep with two new truck tires, 5-gallon containers of gasoline, drinking water, an extra carbine, ammunition and a case of rations (Spam). I found L'Chon Village on the large wall map in my office. It was at least an hour's drive northwest of Masan in mountainous, difficult terrain—known to be guerrilla-infested—and sunset was only 30 minutes away. I had no choice but to leave a note for O'Brien and take off. I was responsible for those men.

When it gets dark in the mountains of Korea, it *really* gets dark! The Korean police had checkpoints set up. They used flags from point-to-point to control the dangerous, winding roads. At each checkpoint the police checked our ID's and looked over our cargo. Without an interpreter it was very difficult, but Casey and I—using sign language and a Korean-English dictionary—got by.

"L-Lieutenant, can I ask a big favor of you?" Casey asked sheepishly.

"Sure, what's that?" I asked back.

"I hate to ask you, sir, but could you p-p-please stop whistling whatever it is you've been whistling over and over again?"

"Sure," I said. But I didn't tell him anything about the tune, "Whenever I am afraid…then no one else will know I'm afraid."

We finally got to the police station. All of the men were safe and enjoying themselves. The Korean police had given them sake (rice wine) to drink and a missionary had brought them food. The missionary and his family lived about a mile away. He and his daughter were getting ready to leave the station as Casey and I drove up. After we met and I thanked him for his help, he invited Casey and me to have dinner and to spend the night at his home. I accepted with all the gratitude I could express. (Whatever his home was, it had to be a thousand times better than that grubby police station.) Casey, though, declined. He found out that the police were bringing some girls to the station.

The missionaries lived in a very nice two-story home located within a fenced and gated compound. The home was attractive, a combination of stone and wood siding. There were rocking chairs all over a large screened-in front porch. Dinner was modest, but well prepared: roasted chicken, vegetables and, of course, rice. The missionary explained that they grew their own food with safe fertilizers and that the water they used came from springs high above the rice-paddy level. He was a Methodist minister from North Carolina. When he and his family decided to do missionary work, they prepared themselves at Scaritt College in Nashville. That gave us plenty to talk about. My room was very comfortable and I slept well. Breakfast consisted of a hot bowl of vegetable soup containing a few slivers of chicken, a bowl of rice, and a helping of strong-smelling "stuff" that looked like rotten vegetables. I had finally come face-to-face with kimche. I'd been hearing about kimche, but had no idea what it was. Well, I learned that kimche was the national dish of Korea. Every family had its own recipe. They mixed a combination of chopped Chinese cabbage, Asian garlic, hot peppers and other vegetable ingredients into a pottery crock. Then they buried the crock, let the ingredients ferment until it was just the way they wanted it (rancid), and ate some of it at every meal. That's what made them all smell like they did—their breath and their perspiration—like Kimche. I thanked my hosts over and over again for their hospitality. They were so gracious. As I was leaving, they asked me to convey their regards to Captain Clark, the Protestant chaplain at the base in Masan.

Casey was in terrible condition, so I drove. The whole team was suffering from hangovers and little, if any, sleep, but we all got back to Masan safely.

◆   ◆   ◆

"Harry, there are a whole lot of things that bother me about Orthodox Judaism," I argued. "Most of all, I simply do not believe that God wrote the Torah word for word and it is, therefore, infallible. I do not think the measure of how 'good' a Jew is should depend on observance of all those many personal practices. It really gripes me to hear one of them say things like, "He's a good Jew; he keeps kosher." Not only are most of the Orthodox prayers irrelevant to me, but some are offensive—like thanking God that they were born a male rather than a female. And I really do not want to move to Jerusalem next year; I want to go home." Harry, of course, had much to say in support of traditional Judaism and much to criticize about Reform, with its lack of requirements and "throwing everything out." This sort of back and forth went on for hours. It was better than sitting in that smoke-filled card room playing one of the many card games going on there day and night.

◆　　　◆　　　◆

Ernie Modarelli was beaming as he reported in. "Lieutenant Pailet, tomorrow I'm going to make a recovery!"

"Great," I responded." Tell me about it."

"The files I've been working on led me to Hill 1675. When we got to the top we found what looked like a foxhole that had been covered up. After we dug around a little bit, we found a bunch of stuff, including this dog tag. It's one of the GI's we were looking for. There were some corroded M-1 rifle parts and a smashed GI-issued canteen. I just know when we get back tomorrow we're going to find some of our guys."

Mr. Lee, Pfc Casey and I left immediately after the last team drove out. We headed for Hill 1675. (Hills were referred to by their height in feet above sea level, as shown on the topographical map.) Modarelli and his team were already at the top, digging into that foxhole. I thought I was in pretty good shape, but I found climbing that steep hill very difficult and painful. My thigh muscles started burning and I was panting so hard I had to stop every few minutes. In the meantime, Mr. Lee went right on up without hesitation. I'd been noticing how the Koreans climbed up hills. They didn't face the hill like Americans did. They climbed up with one side or the other to the hill and their pace was slow but steady. By the time I reached the top the team had already recovered some skeletal remains. They were being as careful as they could possibly be not to unnecessarily disturb anything that might help in making identification. Modarelli took a close-up snap shot each time some new remains were unearthed. When it was time to call it a day and head back we had recovered six skulls and lots of bones. Sorting this out was going to take days. Only one of the skulls was from an American, as far as we could tell. The others had all the signs of having been raised in Asia. By examining the teeth we could tell whether the individual had eaten rice and an Asian diet for many years. The teeth would be ground down in a certain way. Our task was to make field identification, take the remains to the company HQ in Pusan for verification, and then take the likely American remains to the Central Identification Unit (CIU) in Kokura, Japan. The team leader who made the recovery was usually given the option of accompanying the remains to the CIU and answering any questions about the recovery the examiner might ask.

My first recovery—the feeling was indescribable…

5

Murder, POW's and Jacques L'Blanc

The letter from the Judge Advocate General (JAG) began, "You are hereby appointed Pre-Trial Defense Counsel in the Court Marshal case of The United States Army vs. Private Shlomo Abramowitz." The charge: 1st degree murder. The letter went on to provide all sorts of information, instructions, authorizations and forms for me to fill out.

Shlomo Abramowitz (not his real name), as it turned out, was a short, curly-black-haired, Orthodox Jewish nineteen-year-old from Brooklyn. He looked pitiful, curled up in the corner of his prison cell. At first he refused to talk to me, saying over and over again, "I will only talk to a rabbi." Finally, I convinced him I was Jewish (despite my Southern drawl) and was assigned to protect his interest until a JAG (Judge Advocate General) Officer could take over his defense. I assured him that anything he said to me was in strictest confidence; I couldn't even be called to testify. He mumbled something under his breath that sounded like, "*Oy, yoy, yoy.*"

His story: He was the only Caucasian in an otherwise all black QMC Service Company. This Service Company provided the manual labor and guard duty for the salvage yard at the port area of Masan. He hated them and they hated him. They constantly harassed him—ridiculed him and pushed him around. They even stole the things he used for prayer: his yarmulke (skull cap), tallis (prayer shawl) and t'fillin (phylacteries). He got the worst assignments—guard duty from 7-o'clock in the evening until 7-o'clock in the morning. His barracks-mates reported that he was using drugs. His possessions were searched while he was on guard duty. The sergeant claimed he found a cellophane wrapper of heroin under his mattress. Shlomo insisted that someone had planted the wrapper there. They put him under investigation. That night, while on duty, he got an uncontrollable urge to kill. The only person around was his guard partner—a Korean. For no reason, Shlomo started screaming at his partner. He stalked the frightened man, pointed his rifle at him, and chased him around the salvage dump until he shot him. When the wounded man fell, Shlomo kept firing bullets into his body until the other guards ran up and grabbed him, but it was too late to save the guard's life.

When I got back to the post, I found Captain Clark, the Protestant chaplain. (We also had a Catholic chaplain.) First, I told Captain Clark about my experiences with his friends, the missionaries, and their invitation for him to visit. Then I told him about Shlomo. I asked if he knew of any Jewish Chaplains in the area. He said he had heard there was one in Pusan and he would contact him for me.

The next day I went to Shlomo's company HQ. The commander reluctantly allowed me to inspect Shlomo's barracks and to interview the platoon sergeant who claimed he found the heroin. I also interviewed some of Shlomo's barracks mates. I came away convinced that Shlomo's version was probably true. It seemed obvious to me that they had actually tried to frame Shlomo just to get rid of him.

I followed the instructions, filled in the forms, and returned the packet to the JAG office in Pusan. When I heard from the rabbinic chaplain, Shlomo had already been transferred to Pusan for the trial. I later learned that the chaplain, Captain Nathan Estersohn, a Conservative rabbi from Los Angeles, did provide pastoral services to Shlomo throughout his trial. Shlomo was found guilty of the murder—2nd degree rather than 1st degree. The prosecuting JAG officer offered no creditable evidence that the killing was premeditated. The evidence pointed more to factors involving his emotional state of mind. The Jag Officer representing Shlomo did a good job of arguing that the harassment on the part of Shlomo's barracks-mates caused him to "break."

As a result of the contact, the rabbi put me on the mailing list to receive his Bulletin. Each issue included an inspirational message from the rabbi and listed the names and addresses of Jewish GI's in the area. It included the times of religious services, the Torah portion of the week, holidays, and a variety of things he thought would be of interest to his congregation. The rabbi ran an ad in *The Stars and Stripes, Korean Edition,* the weekly newspaper, asking for names and addresses of Jewish members of the UN armed forces, as well as civilians serving in the Department of Defense, the State Department or any other capacity.

I had met the Catholic chaplain through Dick Priest and Ernie Modarelli. The Father put great effort into being priest, mother and father to "his boys" to keep them out of trouble and to urge them to attend Mass. I grew up in a Catholic neighborhood; sometimes my friends took me to Mass with them. I always felt self-conscious and embarrassed when everybody in the church kneeled and I had no choice because I didn't want to make myself conspicuous. Of course when I took my Catholic friends to services with me, I'm sure they felt similarly uncomfortable with parts of our service, especially during those parts of the service involving the congregation in responsive reading. I know, because one of my friends told me he didn't read along with everybody else because he was afraid he'd say the wrong thing.

Captain Clark conducted an interdenominational Protestant service in the post chapel every Sunday morning after the Catholic Mass. He also offered a Bible study class once a week. But he was obviously obsessed with the poverty, pain and suffering that surrounded us. He spent much of his time at orphanages, hospitals, even a lepers' colony, and conducted fund-raisers to help fund his various humanitarian involvements.

◆   ◆   ◆

Captain Clark and I attended the funeral of Shlomo's victim, the Korean guard. We felt that someone from the U.S. Army should pay respects to the family. What I witnessed was diametrically opposite of what we, as children during World War ll, were led to believe about Orientals and their regard for life. The newsreels we saw at the movies showed Japanese soldiers throwing themselves into harm's way without any regard for their own lives. They showed us Japanese pilots flying their planes, filled with explosives, into our battleships and aircraft carriers. The narrators explained that in Asia, human life was totally expendable and that it was a privilege to die for the emperor. I witnessed a lot of fatalities, both in Japan and Korea—vehicle accidents and such. Never did I ever witness the slightest evidence that life was any less worthy amongst the Asians than in America. This Korean family was in profound shock and grief, no different from anyone else's.

◆   ◆   ◆

I finally met David. (I cannot remember his last name.) David was assigned to the Graves Registration section of the United Nations HQ in Teagu. He was only a first lieutenant, but he had high-level responsibilities. It was he who compiled the MIA files and sent them to me. This time he brought them personally. He wanted to meet and discuss the files in person with me. He was eager to go out with a team or two, and frankly, he just wanted to get out of his office for a few days. David had majored in archeology at the University of Denver. David really knew his stuff. He had me critique the status of all of the MIA files the teams were working on. He removed several of the files—those whose names appeared on recently acquired POW lists. Then we reviewed the new files. One of the files in particular caught my attention: Lieutenant Jacques L' Blanc (not real name), West Point, Regular Army (as opposed to Reserve), hometown: New Iberia, LA.

My grandmother (Hattie) and my mother (Sarah) were born and raised in New Iberia. My mother's parents (Theodore and Hattie Alperin) owned a furniture and bric-a-brac business there. After her husband's premature death, Hattie, my mother, and her younger brother Abie moved to New Orleans. They also moved the business and set up shop and residence on Magazine Street. When I played high school football for Newman School we played New Iberia High every year. It was down in Cajun country. Their quarterback had no need to call a huddle. He called the plays right at the line-of-scrimmage, knowing we couldn't understand Cajun French. It's possible I had played against Jacques L'Blanc, or at least had met him. His MIA file indicated that he failed to report in during the hectic retreat near the Hapch'an ferry crossing of the Naktong River. That was not terribly far from Masan, but in an area suspected of being sympathetic to the Communist cause. The people living in several of the villages in that area remained there during the NKPA advance. They provided comfort to the North Koreans. Of course the villagers vehemently denied they did such a thing after the UN forces regained control of the area. I took the L' Blanc file to my quarters for careful study.

◆   ◆   ◆

"Okay, Harry, I admit it looks bad for the southern states to have laws on their books requiring racial segregation. I wish they would repeal those laws tomorrow. If they did, though, I think the races would remain segregated. I was raised in New Orleans, spent three years in Tuscaloosa, Alabama, and have been all over the South. I have seen a lot of the North and lived in New Jersey for eight months. I'd say there is as much segregation one place as the other, except that the colored people seem happier in the South. In the South they sing, have smiles on their faces, and are good-natured. It would be tragic if Congress passed laws forcing the races to integrate. The vast majority of Southern Negroes are not ready for it; their hygiene, their family life, their values, priorities, and their manners are just too different. Right now, the Negro culture is simply not compatible with the white culture."

"All right, if Northerners are genuinely concerned, they could send people down to prepare the blacks for integration. They could start by getting them to bathe regularly and wear clean clothes, to speak understandable English, to get married and live normal family lives. The poorest people on earth can do those things! They could teach things like dependability and responsibility and instill in them how important it is to take school seriously and to get a good education—to get up and do something productive other than laying around breeding. The USA can afford to help them in a way that will work in the long run rather than jam integration down the South's throat; that will never work."

"Sure, Harry, there are many exceptions. My dad hired Bruce as a porter. Bruce had a desire to better himself. My dad taught Bruce to become a jewelry polisher. To be a good polisher in a jewelry making and repair shop takes more skill than you'd think, and the polisher must be impeccably honest. Bruce mastered the trade and he earned enough to purchase his own home and to send his children to college."

"You're right; Lt. Edwards could fit in anywhere. He was raised in an advantaged situation. His family has lived in New Jersey for generations, owns a string of funeral homes—*black* funeral homes. Edwards attended a *black* college and lives in a predominately *black* neighborhood. In fact, as far as neighborhoods are concerned, New Orleans is more integrated than Northern cities. The city has a great number of *Creoles* (mixed-blooded descendants from the West Indies) speaking so many different dialects that nobody knows just what they are."

◆   ◆   ◆

Dick Priest took great delight in giving me shocking news. "Lieutenant, there's been a POW uprising and breakout. A lot of the NKPA and Chinese prisoners escaped. The Marines rounded up most of them. They killed some of the POWs and one Marine got killed."

"That's terrible," I said, "Where did all this happen?"

"The POW Camp not far from here on the coast toward Chinhae. Captain Welsh has arranged for a helicopter to pick you up so you can survey the situation and decide how to handle it."

The Bell helicopter was a little two-seater with a Plexiglas bubble. It did not have doors; you just strapped yourself in. When it surged upward, I felt like my stomach stayed on the ground—the same feeling when as a kid I went up in an elevator. It was the opposite feeling going down. The first thing I saw were recaptured POWs sitting in the camp yard. They were sitting in *formation* so they could be controlled and counted. I say "sitting" because Koreans, I noticed, rest in a squatting position—like a baseball catcher. You'd see them squatting like that at bus stops; you'd see them sitting around in a circle shooting the bull in that position. It's the same position one must assume to use an Eastern-style commode (the bowl is recessed into the floor), or the position three-year-old girls get into while playing with their dolls. Most GI's, including me, were terribly uncomfortable in that position; Koreans could squat like that for hours at a time—even the papa-sans.

Figure 18—Processing recaptured POW's

A POW camp officer and a Marine captain greeted me. I told them we would pick up the deceased in the morning and take them to my company HQ at the UNMC in Pusan for processing and disposition. The Marine captain asked a lot of questions about the process and was especially interested in the notification—what the family of the deceased Marine would be told, etc. I answered the best I could. He was tough, but appreciative. Then he invited me to come to their Officers' Club on any Saturday night. That's when they had entertainment. The 2nd Marine Division just happened to be located near the POW Camp. The 1st Marine Division was in the combat zone where they were engaged in heavy fighting. Secretary of State Dulles was starting to suggest cease-fire talks. This sparked acceleration in the fighting. Both sides were making a fierce effort to end up with the most advantageous territory. The 2nd Marine Division was in reserve and spent its time training and sending replacements up to the 1st. They were also responsible for helping the POW camp commander on an as-needed basis.

◆   ◆   ◆

It was a beautiful Saturday morning. Pfc. Casey was on weekend pass. I said, "Kim let's go for a ride in the country." We loaded the jeep with all the usual and took off toward the town of Ch'angyung and the ferry crossing near Hapch'an. The Korean countryside fascinated me, and I was interested in how they grew rice. I watched the farmers plow, fertilize, and prepare their paddies. Meanwhile, green rice seedlings were growing in the seedling beds. When the seedlings were ready to be transplanted into the paddies, the farmers took handfuls of the seedlings in bunches and distributed them at careful and consistent distances throughout the paddies. One male farmer got on one side of a paddy and one got on the opposite side. Each held a pole. A cord that stretched across the paddy connected the poles. The cord had little tufts tied at row-width distances. When all that was ready, the mama-sans and daughter-sans came out in shorts and barefooted. They sloshed into the paddy. Each stood behind one of the little tuffs along the cord, picked up a bunch of seedlings and planted one seedling under "her" tuft. After that row was planted, the farmers moved to the next row, and so forth (like when a football team makes a first down and the officials move the markers) until the paddy was covered with bright green rice seedlings in a perfect grid pattern.

Figure 19—Planting rice seedlings

Ch'angyung was the cleanest and most attractive Korean town I had yet seen. Saturday was market day. It was also the day they held a big oxen auction. I parked the jeep so Kim and I could walk around and watch the auction. At the same time, it gave the villagers an opportunity to look us over and try to figure us out. I sensed that they feared me. Of course, I was wearing a holster with a loaded 45, and there were the rifles in the jeep—hardly overtures of "Let's be friends." Kim picked up on the situation and struck up conversations with several of the papa-sans in the crowd. They seemed friendly, so I told Kim to ask if they knew where the fighting had taken place around here because my job was to try to find American soldiers who had become lost during the fighting. Even though I couldn't understand a word they said, I could sense that they were reluctant to be forthcoming. Then I remembered the lecture on how to conduct yourself in any kind of transaction with Asians: "Take it easy, do not rush things, and build confidence—one layer at a time." So with big smiley good-byes, I took Kim by the hand to stroll up and down the isles of the marketplace.

Figure 20—Oxen auction in Ch'angyung

Figure 21—Market day in Ch'angyung

What I found amazing was the variety of things they made from beer cans: cups, pans, flint guns, and other useful items. There was an abundance of fresh produce—all the ingredients for making kimche and soup. There was smelly fish, chickens, and awful-looking red meat. Some of the stalls were devoted to traditional Korean clothing and others to over-the-counter items and cosmetics, which had obviously found their way from the Army PX. I bought a few things, like a pair of those Korean-style rubber shoes to wear in the shower, and a flint gun for Harry and me to use in our quarters. (Mosquito season was upon us.)

Figure 22—THP buying flint gun

Kim wasn't interested in the shopping, so he went to watch a puppet show. I was shocked when I realized that the puppet show was really communistic propaganda. "Uncle Sam" was the villain and the victims were Korean peasants, led by a puppet that resembled Mao Tse Tung. I later learned that puppet shows like this traveled all over non-communistic Asia, like South Korea, the Philippines, and Indonesia. They set up on market day in rural areas. The plots were simple and designed to influence the illiterate mind toward communistic ideology. For example, scene one would show "Uncle Sam" exploiting the villagers in some way. In scene two, the poor villagers were suffering as a result of the exploitation. In scene three, the heroes, Mao Tse Tung or General Il Suk Kim of North Korea would defeat "Uncle Sam" and rescue the villagers, who were appreciative and forever beholding.

The weather had been pretty all day, but dark clouds were beginning to gather. I heard thunder off in the distance. There were several streams to ford on the way back to Masan, so I tore Kim away from the puppet show. The Hapch'an ferry crossing would have to wait.

Shortly after we left I took a wrong turn. The road I took wound up a steep hill and led me onto a desolate, rocky plateau. Off in the distance I recognized three very rusty U. S. Army tanks. Apparently they had been disabled and abandoned during the fighting three years ago. The fact that the Koreans had not cultivated this area led me to believe that this must be a mine field. I noted the location on my map, turned the jeep around—careful to stay within the roadbed—and headed for Masan.

During the drive back I thought, "How easy it would have been during the vicious fighting for a GI to desert his unit and vanish into these hills. He could have easily found refuge in one of these villages, and could still be hiding out. He could have decided to join the North Korean guerrillas. Who knows?" I also gave serious thought to the planning of my next visit to the area.

Back in Masan, I reported the abandoned tanks to Ordinance. They were appreciative and said they would send a tank retriever to bring them back.

At dinner that night I told Harry all about my adventure to Ch'angyong. He said he thought he would enjoy going out with me sometime. I told him that since Casey and most of my men were on weekend pass I was planning to drive to the Hapch'an ferry crossing tomorrow (Sunday) morning with Kim, and I invited Harry to come along.

Dinner at the Top of the Mark was usually pretty good. The meals were well-balanced and the service (Korean young women) was surprisingly good. The Quartermaster Corp (QMC) processed all the food items in the States (canned, dehydrated, dry-packed). Nothing was fresh except for the tomatoes; the QMC grew them in hydroponics farms in Japan. The cooks could only use what the QMC sent them from Pusan, and they were required to follow the published menu schedule. Every menu—breakfast, lunch and dinner—called for potatoes. You cannot imagine how many different ways there are to prepare potatoes. On one occasion the Quartermaster ran out of potatoes! They substituted macaroni into the meal plan. We had macaroni three times a day for three weeks. The cooks followed the meal plan. We had macaroni mashed, boiled, fried, au gratin, scalloped, hash brown, baked and stuffed. After that I couldn't look at macaroni, much less eat it.

After dinner it was always card playing time at the Top of the Mark. You had your choice of any number of games: poker, bridge, gin rummy, hearts, pinochle, cribbage or backgammon. I introduced the Cajun game of *buray,* which was a big gambling game. They loved it—anything to break the monotony. But, in fact, I didn't play cards that much; I always seemed to have enough to keep me busy in my quarters. Louise sent a steady stream of newsy letters and I wrote about my day every day. She subscribed to the *New York Times* for me, which kept me informed on what was really going on, rather than having to rely on *The Stars and Stripes—Korean Edition*.

This particular night Harry and I went back to our quarters to mosquito-proof our end of the BOQ. The Post Quartermaster had issued mosquito netting for each of us to drape around our bunk. Harry and I, though, occupied the end of the Quonset, so we rigged the netting in the corridor from floor to ceiling, wall to wall. Since we had two nets, we double protected, creating a vestibule. Then we tried out the flint gun I had bought at the market by spraying inside our area. It worked! I could hardly wait for my next visit…

6

Patient Bargaining

What fun! Two weekends in a row Harry, Kim and I went to the Hapch'an area. We discovered a beautiful little beach along the Naktong River near the ferry crossing. We took picnic lunches that the mess sergeant had prepared for us, along with bathing suits, a Scrabble game, and a big blanket to spread out on the beach. We took the risk that the river was safe for swimming. The villagers became comfortable with our presence. They even huddled around us to watch us play Scrabble. Outings like these were relaxing and a welcomed relief from our daily routines. Besides, it was a way to bolster confidence with the villagers.

Figure 23—Ferry crossing Naktong River at Hapch'an

Figure 24—Harry & THP playing Scrabble on the beach

Figure 25—Kim & THP at the beach

Out of the blue, a Korean teenager approached Kim and asked Kim to go with him to meet his Papa-san. When Kim returned, he said,"Rutenant, Papa-san want to speak you." I went with Kim and met the Papa-san. His appearance was typical of the Papa-sans I had noticed ever since I arrived in Korea. He was wearing the long, white goatee and the long, white cotton kimono, and a top hat made of black horsehair. He was holding a long, skinny pipe with a tiny little bowl for smoking whatever they smoked. It turned out that this Papa-san was the village master of a nearby village. He explained (through Kim) that the village elders wanted to meet with me privately. Encouraged, I said, "Kim, ask him when they want to meet and find out how we can contact him when we come back."

A few days later, at the appointed time and place, Kim and I entered the hut where the village leaders met. Six leaders, all stereotypical Papa-sans—all smoking their pipes—were sitting crossed-legged on floor mats. It was painful for me; I suffered without letting on; but I got down in that same position and sat as erect as I could. First, there was small talk—lots of it. "Where was my home?" "Tell about my family?" "Why I become GI?" "Where did Kim come from?" "Where his family?" Then one asked, "Why we search for GI's?" That question gave me the opportunity to inject some emotion into the discussion. I replied by emphasizing that GI's were here risking their lives to keep South Koreans free people and not slaves to Communist leaders. I described GI's mama-san, papa-san, wife and baby, worrying about what happened to their loved one. I tried to get them to agree how terrible it must be not to know whether your loved one is dead or a prisoner.

Then one of the elders told a story. It went like this: "When NKPA come down from north, villagers afraid of NKPA. All villagers go to Pusan. After fighting stop, villagers come back to village. They bury many dead soldiers—some NKPA, some ROK, some American GI."

"Why," I asked," they not tell Army?"

"They afraid tell Army," the elder answered.

"Why they afraid?" I pressed.

"They afraid Army think they not leave village when NPKA come and they help Communist," he replied.

I asked if they knew where American GI's were buried. From the translated conversation I could not tell whether there were more than one GI. They explained that a member of the village—a rice farmer—claimed he knew where GI was buried. The problems were he did not want anyone to know who he was and he did not want anyone to know where GI was (or were) buried. The reason was, as it turned out, he buried GI where he found GI…in one of his rice paddies. Not only did he not want to be identified, but what's more, he did not want my trucks driving through his rice paddies, nor did he want a recovery team digging in them

After a lengthy and frustrating negotiation, which involved one of the elders periodically leaving the hut to go consult with the mystery farmer, we finally reached an agreement. 1) I would *not* report this to "Army." 2) I would return next Saturday with only Kim. 3) Farmer would disinter remains and get them ready for me to make a field ID to satisfy myself that the remains were American. 4) I would bring a large sack of Korean rice to compensate the farmer for disturbing his rice crop (and a large sack for the village elders). It had to be Korean rice. To them, rice grown elsewhere was inferior.

◆   ◆   ◆

"Casey, I need two large sacks of Korean rice—number one grade. I need them for this Saturday,"

He could tell by my voice that I was serious. All he said was, "Lieutenant, I'll need your beer allotment and a carton of cigarettes—maybe more. I'll try those and let you know."

Pfc. Casey knew people who knew their way around the black market. Obviously, many of the items that supplied the black market somehow found their way out of the Post Exchange (PX). The PX was where the authorized personnel bought our toiletries, magazines, cigarettes, beer, cameras, film, and other such items. PX prices were "at cost"—extremely reasonable. For instance, a carton of cigarettes cost us $1.00 and a case of beer $4.00 ($1.00 a six-pack). There were two catches: the first was we were only allotted two cartons of cigarettes and one case of beer a week. The other catch was that we couldn't always get the brand we wanted. That may sound like a lot of beer, but remember, we couldn't drink the water; besides, the Army required a reduced alcohol content. I smoked one carton of cigarettes a week; a case of beer lasted me a month (the Scotch was reasonable too), but I bought my full allotment of cigarettes and beer every week. I gave the extra carton and case to Casey, and the next day he would bring me $8.00 to $9.00 (Military Scrip) for the carton and $14.00 to $16.00 for the case of beer. Not only did the prices fluctuate daily, but also it mattered how the brands rated in the polls. For example, the No.1 brand of cigarettes might bring $9.00, No.2, $8.00, and so on. Usually, No.1 was either Camels or Lucky Strike, with Chesterfields and Phillip Morris 3rd and 4th. The beers were usually Budweiser (1st), Schlitz (2d), and Miller High Life (3rd).

It was a very busy week for me. I studied all of the MIA files of those reported missing in the Hapch'an area. The thought of recovering Jacques L' Blanc, of course, gave me a rush of anxiety. Mr. Lee, my official interpreter, insisted that I go with him to Chinhae. His grandson had reached his first birthday and the family celebration was scheduled for Sunday at noon. On top of that, Captain Welsh was trying to order me to Pusan for a staff meeting and I kept telling him (all of this through Private Pierce and his radio full of static) how important it was for me to be here over the weekend. Nevertheless, in my letters to Louise I alerted her to the news that there was a possibility I would be in Pusan, maybe even Japan, in about ten days and would attempt to get an overseas telephone call through to her.

◆   ◆   ◆

I experienced enormous satisfaction each time one of my S & R teams made a recovery, but the thought of making this particular recovery on my own under such unusual circumstances promised to be even more satisfying.

The level of excitement increased as Kim and I approached the village near Hapch'an. The Papa-sans were waiting for us. They were guarding the remains—four of them—all meticulously arranged as best they could. One of the skulls had a dog tag lodged between its upper and lower teeth. Upon closer examination, it was positively American. Its teeth were straight and well cared for, with both mercury and gold fillings. The name on the dog tag was not L' Blanc, but something like Reynolds, and it matched one of the MIA files. There was no guarantee, of course, that the dog tag belonged to those remains. Two of the remains were definitely 100% Asian, and one was too difficult for me to make a confident decision.

Every GI was issued and required to wear a dog tag around his neck. It was made of non-corrosive metal and embossed with his name, serial number, blood type, and religion ("C" for Christian, "H" for Hebrew, "M" for Moslem, etc.). That helped Graves Registration know, for instance, whether to use a Cross, a Star of David, or a Crescent & Star, for the grave marker. The dog tag was sized just right and notched to help secure it between the teeth for ID purposes.

I left the two sacks of rice and took all the remains back to Masan. Before I left, I did my best to reach an understanding that I could return and recover any more GI's that anyone else knew about. The Papa-sans promised they would ask all villagers to try to *remember* and to contact me if there was any hope.

◆   ◆   ◆

I had the PX gift wrap a baby gift, and on Sunday Mr. Lee and I drove to Chinhae for the birthday party. Mr. Lee had invited my driver, Pfc. Casey, but he had other things on his mind for the weekend. Chinhae was located on the coast southeastwardly of Masan and was the headquarters for the Korean Navy. On the way there was a tunnel through one of the many rugged hills. Mr. Lee explained that American POWs of the Japanese built the tunnel as forced laborers during

World War II. He suggested that some day we spend some time searching the area. "Maybe we find remains. Maybe dog tags."

The birthday party was much more elaborate than I had imagined. Mr. Lee had a very large family, and the parents had lots of friends. Everybody showed up. The baby was all dressed up in a handmade, satin-looking Korean kimono. I was the only American. They had the most bountiful and colorful display of Korean foods I had ever seen. However, serious words were spoken before anyone ate. The Koreans celebrated a child surviving its first year like we celebrate a birth. The infant mortality rates were so high they didn't give the baby a name or consider the infant as a member of the family until it survived the first year—thus the big celebration.

My problem was how to handle the food situation. I did not want to offend anyone, especially Mr. Lee. Fortunately, they had shrimp. The shrimp were pink, which indicated to me that they had been boiled. They also had open flames and bamboo skewers for roasting bite-sized pieces of meat, fish, poultry and some of the vegetables—none of which I could identify. So, I peeled and roasted the shrimp. When one of the women insisted I try something she thought I would enjoy, I just put it on my plate and thanked her.

After we left the party, Mr. Lee showed me a beautiful monument near the center of town. It was a memorial to a young Korean girl. She had been a selected concubine of the commanding general of the area during the Japanese occupation. As the story went, the general and the girl were out for a romantic walk one moonlit night along the edge of a cliff high above the sea. He grabbed at her for a big hug, but she thrust herself at him with such force that both of them fell to their deaths into the sea.

◆   ◆   ◆

Casey asked if Marvin G. could go in his place to Pusan. I agreed. I liked Marvin G. He was a team leader—a mild, easygoing corporal. He had a master's degree in some scientific field. Even though he was a team leader, he insisted on doing all the team's driving. Marvin G. was the only member of the platoon, other than Casey, that I would trust to drive me to Pusan. So he drove and I sat with a 30-caliber carbine in my lap. Marvin G. was planning to spend his time in Pusan shopping. He had a list of things that members of the platoon had given him to buy—mostly gifts for their girlfriends. The cargo (the four carefully wrapped remains and our luggage) was in the rear of the jeep. Thundershowers slowed us down. It took most of the day to drive that horrible road to Pusan. We

arrived late in the afternoon. Captain Welsh, a newly arrived ROTC 2nd Lieutenant, and a Turkish Army Captain were waiting for my arrival before starting
cocktail hour. I was splattered with mud. Welsh asked me if I was still a Scotch
man. By the time the houseboy brought my things into the BOQ and I had
washed up and changed clothes, the drinks were poured. I sensed something was
going on. Welsh introduced me to the new lieutenant, John Dortch, and the
Turkish Captain, whose name was too difficult to pronounce so they called him
Garcia—I guess because he had a full, black, Spanish-looking, handlebar mustache. Garcia was a liaison from the Turkish Army to the UNMC. He was a
handsome lady's man, very likable and good company. He oversaw the two
Turkish enlisted men who were quartered at the 114th. Their job was to take care
of the Turkish graves and any new Moslem deceased by praying five times a day
at their graves.

Then Welsh offered a really nice toast to my S & R efforts. When I raised my
glass, I noticed that there were some strange-looking, glistening objects in my
drink. The things turned out to be silver bars. Welsh had frozen them in the ice
cubes. I had been promoted to 1st Lieutenant! I was excited and felt good about
it, even though the promotion was pretty much automatic after sixteen months
or so. At least it gave us a good reason to celebrate.

Later, after dinner and after Garcia had left, Welsh revealed to me that he had
applied for emergency transfer back to the States. His wife had been diagnosed
with an advanced malignant growth. He said his replacement had been selected
and was somewhere in the pipeline. Actually, he was about due to rotate back
anyway, but it was sad about his wife.

◆   ◆   ◆

Welsh had arranged for me to accompany the recovered MIA remains to the
Central Identification Unit (CIU) in Kokura, Japan. He arranged for me to fly
out of K-9 airport (a US Air Corps air strip located about three miles west of the
UNMC) on a cargo plane that was returning to Fukuoka airport after delivering
a load of hydroponically grown tomatoes to K-9. The plane shuttled back and
forth two or three times a week. The pilots were happy to have some company to
break the monotony. The interior cargo compartment was absolutely cavernous.
I sat in a jump seat near the pilots, but it was much too noisy to carry on any kind
of meaningful conversation.

CIU sent a jeep and driver (Japanese) to meet me and take me to the CIU to
process the remains. The CIU was awesome. The processing and examining area

looked like a very long warehouse lined with examining slabs. The building was well lit and ventilated, but not enough to eliminate the strong odor of wintergreen. The remains were kept in refrigerated compartments which lined the sidewalls, and only the remains being examined were out on the examining tables. The place was very sterile, and almost everything was stark white. The examiners wore white surgical gowns, masks and gloves. They worked in teams composed of medical, dental, physiology, anthropological, fingerprint and other experts. When any member of the U.S. Military was reported as MIA, the Defense Department requested all sorts of information from the next of kin such as dental records, physicians reports (especially orthopedic reports and x-rays of broken bones), and pictures showing birth marks or unusual characteristics. These were added to the MIA files. All together, it seemed like one gigantic jigsaw puzzle. I was told that the CIU would never give up attempting to make a positive ID, no matter how hopeless it appeared. There was always the hope that new information, technology or discoveries would come along.

After the processing and the tour, I was shown to my quarters and instructed how to make use of the motor pool of jeeps with drivers so I could go into town and arrange to be picked up. I did a little research on the best place to go for dinner and went. It turned out to be a combination restaurant and bathhouse. Only U.S. Military officers and Japanese businessmen were allowed, but it was different than the clubs in Tokyo. Each customer was assigned a hostess, of course. The hostess assigned to me was bossy and matter-of-fact. She announced, "First have drink, relax in lounge, then chop-chop, then I bathe you." Dinner was served family-style around a large, very low table. We sat on the floor crossed-legged. The food was not memorable. The bath was in a large tiled room where everyone went after finishing their meal. All the customers were nude except the hostesses, who wore white shorts. We went through the usual Japanese bath routine, the difference being that it was communal. My driver was punctual and I was glad to leave that place.

I went into town the next morning. I walked around the busy town center, just soaking in the scene. The first stop I made was the overseas telephone center in hopes of getting a call through to Louise. The place was crowded with GI's, but I was told all connections to the States were down and to check again tomorrow. I had brought my shopping list with me and tried to spot shops that were likely to carry the kinds of things on my list. One thing caught my attention more than anything else in the city: the Nortake China factory with its own display store. I remember my mother having Nortake china—"Made in Japan." The store was huge and displayed the entire line of china that was made there. I bought several things and had them shipped to Louise. The best thing was a tea-dessert set. It had gray, modernist, amoebic designs with a pretty yellow background. I thought the set was really neat. I remember the day as being very pleasant, even though I passed up a hand-carved ivory chess set I knew I would regret. Really, the only disagreeable thing was the many GI's on R&R. They were having lots of fun, but it was annoying in an embarrassing way to see them acting so crude and rude. It reminded me of the way the drunken Aussie enlisted men acted in Kure.

The following morning I returned to the CIU. They complimented me on the recovery, especially the obvious American-raised Caucasian. They kept one of the others for further study. It could have been an Oriental U.S. GI raised in Hawaii or California. They asked me to return the obvious (to them) Asian-raised for burial at the UNMC. They showed me some sutle ways to distinguish between those raised in North Korea or Manchuria and those raised in South Korea. There were certain characteristics affected by the dietary differences.

The cargo plane was loaded with tomatoes. I sat in my jump seat. Funny, I was happy to be going "home".

◆   ◆   ◆

Welsh insisted on teaching me details of administrating the affairs of the UNMC. He was preparing me to take over if it became necessary. The UNMC was very busy. The negotiators at Panmunjon were trying to reach a cease-fire agreement and arrange some sort of truce. As a result, the number of deceased was noticeably less, but it was still considerable. In addition, Welsh was beginning to receive requests that certain remains be disinterred and repatriated to their country. Also, he could not be sure his replacement would arrive in time to be oriented before his orders to return stateside came through. In that event, he wanted someone prepared to take over the 114th the minute he had the opportunity to leave. That meant I was there two extra days.

Each night Welsh made plans for us, along with Garcia and Dortch, to go out for a good dinner. The first night we went to the Chinese Embassy. It was in downtown Pusan in a drab four-story building. The Communist Chinese operated their embassy there, even after the Chinese Army had entered the war on the side of the North Koreans. But when General Douglas MacArthur pulled that brilliant Inchon Invasion and sent the Chinese Army and the NKPA into retreat, the Chinese Embassy officials refused to return to China. Instead, they converted the embassy building into a restaurant. The food was authentic and excellent.

The next night we went to Tongnae Springs. This was a natural mineral hot springs resort about nine miles north of Pusan. The medicinal benefits had been known and enjoyed by the Koreans for many centuries. The Japanese though, during their 40-odd-year occupation, developed the amenities for the exclusive use of Japanese Military Officers. Now it was used by UN Military Officers, Department of Defense (DOD) civilian personnel, and Koreans who could afford the prices. A charming Korean inn nestled in the trees was the central feature. All of the buildings were constructed of rough honed wood with thatched roofs (some of the few wooden structures I had seen in Korea—probably imported by the Japanese). There were two good-sized buildings—one for the hot springs therapy and one for dining. In addition, there were cabins for overnight guests. All of them surrounded a Japanese garden and a small lake. The menu was very limited, but whatever you ordered was especially good. My favorite was the fried butterfly shrimp. I couldn't get enough of them. Of course the hot bath and massage before dinner and the scotch helped build up my appetite. Garcia became the life of the party. After a few drinks he became totally uninhibited and simply followed his instincts. He wooed one of the Korean waitresses and spent the night with her.

The following morning, a courier brought Captain Welsh a message that some VIPs were on their way to visit the UNMC. Walsh wanted me to learn how to properly receive them. He reviewed all of the routine and protocol involved in such a visit. First, I had to dress-up; so did everyone else that would take part in the visit. They arrived on schedule. The VIPs were Walter Robinson, President Ike's Special Truce Envoy, U.S. Ambassador to the ROK, Briggs, and several generals. I learned how to lead them through the paths leading to the UN flag and to help place the floral wreath in the right spot for picture taking. Right behind the UN flag were the graves of three unknown soldiers. One of the generals asked me why we didn't put their names on the markers like all the others.

Figure 26—VIP's Walter Robertson & Ambassador Briggs

After the visit, I got the opportunity to drive into downtown Pusan and go to the telephone company building where I could again try to place an overseas call to Louise. I put my name on the list and waited my turn. After an hour or so my name was called. The procedure was to give the calling information in writing to a Korean clerk. The clerk would try to get the call through to an operator in San Francisco, then that operator would attempt to call an operator in Nashville, who would put in the call to Louise. The attempts went on and on with no success. Ultimately, I had to abandon this attempt and hope for further opportunities.

Figure 27—THP getting boot shine in downtown Pusan

Marvin G. and I were now ready for the awful drive back to Masan, with the jeep packed with the variety of things he had shopped for in Pusan and the few things I brought back from Japan…

7

Winding Down Masan

Finally—we got away from the 114th HQ and out of the congestion of Pusan.

During the long drive back to Masan, Marvin G. and I got involved in an unusually intimate conversation, despite the potholes and hairpin turns. It all started when I asked if he had been to Japan. When he said "No," I asked, "Are you interested in going on R & R?"

His answer was, "Not really."

I went on to describe how quaint it was there…a completely different culture. The people—so industrious and so advanced compared to the Koreans—who had been forced to live under Japanese occupation for fifty years. I rambled on, sharing my thoughts on the similarity of the Japanese and the Germans. Both seemed to have built-in characteristics to strive for excellence and national superiority—sooo different from the South Koreans, who appeared happiest just sitting around philosophizing. I gave examples. In Japan, if you asked someone like a waiter a simple request like, "May I have a glass of milk?" or an employee in a store, "Can I get this gift-wrapped?" you could depend on it being done promptly and perfectly. If you asked the Japanese clerk "Where is the gift department?" The clerk would personally take you there. Korean employees, on the other hand, don't seem to understand or care that you want it done *now,* not sometime in the future; it might get done today, tomorrow or next week. That is probably the result of the Japanese military occupation and oppression. Then I described how much fun the GIs on R&R had. The Army prearranged for each of them to have a Japanese hostess for the five days they were there. The hostesses had to be members of the *White Lily Society.* That meant they had to speak adequate English, be trained as guides and carry a *White Lily Society Card.* The cards had to show that they had been tested for venereal disease (VD) on a weekly basis and were totally free of any infection. Marvin G. told me he liked the Koreans, but he didn't care about the Japanese or going there. He said, "I'm just happy spending my free time with Yonglee."

That was the first time I ever heard of Yonglee. I asked him to tell me about her. "Lieutenant, please promise me you'll keep this to yourself," He said. I promised.

"I went to a cherry blossom fair in Satch'on. I went by myself. This was a week or so before Lt. Edwards drove to Pusan to get you. At that time I was the only GI in the platoon who spent nights in the platoon headquarters on the base, and I was lonely. I was also afraid of getting VD. There were lots of young Koreans—high school age—at the fair. After I was there for a while, a few of them came up to me. They wanted to practice their English. It was all very innocent. I don't know what hit me, but I was attracted to this one girl. I couldn't get my eyes off of her: the glistening, jet-black hair, the rosy cheeks, those slanted but twinkling eyes." (Actually, their eyes are *not* slanted. The Koreans, as well as other Orientals, are born with extra fatty tissue above and below their eye lids. This gives the appearance of their eyes being slanted. The excess tissue can be removed surgically, and some who could afford it had their eyes "Westernized.") "She seemed to enjoy me staring at her. Before I realized it, the festivities of the fair faded into the background. We paired off, walked over to a bench, then sat and talked and talked. She was smart and had a great personality. Almost everyone else had left the fair."

"All of a sudden Yonglee got this scared look on her face, like she had seen a ghost. She cried out, 'Papa-san, papa-san, no, no, Papa-san, Papa-san!' Then she started running and I tried my best to follow along behind her. It was real dark, but she knew her way. She ran through alleys and made a zillion turns until she got to her home. Her Papa-san was outside, waiting for her. He started yelling and screaming in Korean. I don't think he saw me. He started beating on Yonglee and grabbed her hair and dragged her into the house."

"I don't know how I found my way back to the base, but I finally made it. Sach'on isn't all that big, but it is very congested. The next morning a Korean security guard woke me up. He made me follow him to the front gate. I thought I had done something wrong by coming in so late the night before. Yonglee was there. She had her things with her. Her Papa-san had kicked her out of the house and said he never wanted to see her again."

That was the custom in traditional Korean families. If a daughter had just one date with an American GI, they would disown her.

"When Lt. Edwards showed up, I told him what had happened. He said, 'Don't get so upset. That's happened to a lot of the GI's in the platoon. Take the day off, go find a hutchie and move your girl in. Then you'll have some place to go at night.'"

"Well, she followed me to Masan. Now, Lieutenant—you promise me this is all confidential—right?" I gave him my assurance. "Yonglee and I are going to have a baby."

I had been noticing young, pretty, Korean women wearing Sears Roebuck Catalog clothing and make-up with babies that were obviously Eurasian or Afrasian. I would see them around the market places doing their shopping and errands with the child strapped to their backs, papoose-style. I never thought I would ever be confronted with such a situation. "Marvin G.," I asked, "what are you going to do?"

He quickly replied, "I'm going to marry Yonglee and get her and my baby back to the States."

I assured Marvin G. I would cooperate and sign any required forms. I said that, even though I had heard that the Army strongly disapproved and made such a plan practically impossible for a GI to accomplish.

Figure 28—Eurasian baby

◆   ◆   ◆

Back in Masan, O'Brien reported that a South African fighter pilot had slammed into a hilltop in a desolate area near the town of Chonju, about 70 miles northwest of Masan. That was heavily infested guerrilla territory. He sent Modarelli's team with a ROK Police escort to make the recovery. He estimated that it would take several days, and he obviously expected me to be proud of his decision. I wasn't. Inwardly I was petrified. Next he told me about the tank retriever that had hit a land mind. The explosion caused the boom to swing around, killing one of the crew and injuring two others. When he told me that the incident occurred at a creek crossing about a mile south of Ch'angnyung, I knew exactly where it happened. That's where we went to the oxen auction on the way to Hapch'an ferry crossing. I knew the creek where it had happened. The bridge had been blown up during the fighting, and all traffic had to ford the creek. There was a well-worn route that everybody followed. Harry, Kim and I had forded that creek in my jeep eight or ten times. The weight of the tank retriever, tragically, caused the mine to explode. Ordinance had sent the crew to retrieve the tanks that I had reported to them. O'Brien also informed me that Harry Martin had been promoted to 1st Lt. and had been transferred to Taegu. "Otherwise," he said, "everything went routinely." He handed me all my accumulated mail and I had plenty of letter writing catching up in front of me.

Dick Priest and Kim, however, were all excited when they saw me. Kim gave me a big hug—happy to see his "Pop." Priest gave me the news that a group of famous cartoonists would be here in Masan in a day or two. They were on a tour of South Korea, arranged by the DOD. The purpose of the tour was to have this group of talented cartoonists attempt to capture the considerable sense of humor that prevailed amongst the UN Forces despite the savagery of this war. They wanted me to show them what the Pusan Perimeter was like and to expose them to the work of Search and Recovery. When they arrived and were introduced, I recognized each of them for his particular cartoon. I grew up reading the comic strips that appeared in the Sunday newspaper, so I was familiar with the cartoons that my guests created. There was Cliff Rogerson ("Francis the Talking Mule"); Al Posen ("Sweeney & Son"); Jeff Hayes ("Chip") and ("Silent Sam"); and Elmer R. Messer, editorial cartoonist for *The Rochester Times-Union*. We spent two days together, and it was definitely a highlight of my life. They were real cut-ups and found interest and humor in almost everything they saw.

Figure 29—Visiting Cartoonists

However, they were noticeably uncomfortable when we encountered student demonstrations going on in Masan and in some of the towns we drove through on our tour. The students were furious with the way the Panmunjon negotiations were going. The students opposed a divided Korea. They blamed Syngman Rhee, the beleaguered first president of the Republic of South Korea, for not invading the North to unite their country. Many Korean families were separated and unable to communicate with, much less visit each other.

This division between north and south had existed ever since the Japanese surrender on August 14, 1945. The Soviet Union entered the war against the Japanese the same day the United States dropped the second atomic bombs on Nagasaki, just five days before the Japanese surrender. Somehow President Roosevelt agreed to let the Soviets accept the Japanese surrender north of the 38th parallel while the Japanese surrendered to us south of the 38th. This turned out to be the beginning of an on-going misfortune.

◆   ◆   ◆

Boy was I relieved to see Modarelli and his team drive up with smiles on their faces. The mission was a success. They found what was left of the pilot in the charred wreckage of the plane, which had burned badly upon impact. The remains weighed about six pounds and hardly any of the pilot's personal effects survived. Modarelli made a detailed report of the recovery and his experiences in the Chonju area. His report was so shocking, I asked him to write out his entire report. Part of his report included what the team witnessed in the center of town. The ROK Police had set a trap for a band of North Korean guerillas. The guerillas had been raiding some of the villages in the area—stealing rice, chickens, pigs and other food. During one raid they kidnapped a teenage girl, then raped and killed her. The ROK police trap worked. They captured two of the guerillas and killed the rest. When they brought the prisoners back to Chonju, a mob of townspeople overpowered the police, grabbed the prisoners, beheaded them and began playing soccer with the heads before the police could regain control of the situation. Modarelli asked if he could please take the South African remains to the CIU in Kokura. I happily granted permission.

Not long after that, two major events occurred: first, the Panmunjon negotiators entered into a signed agreement; and second, Captain Paul Jackson Rucker succeeded Captain Welsh as company commander of the 114th. No one was happy about either event. Of all the Captains in the U.S. Army, I had to get Paul Jackson Rucker! He taught the course in infantry tactics at the Officers Training School at Fort Lee, VA. All of us who were unfortunate enough to take his course were turned off by his caustic style and condescending attitude. He delighted in "putting you down." Rucker had attended military academies all through school and was a West Point graduate. He was regular army all the way, and a terribly frustrated and bitter individual. He had already graduated from the Point when the war started. He had volunteered for and was on his way to a combat assignment when the plane he was on crashed. He was the only survivor; he suffered some burns and a mangled leg. Captain Rucker spent months in the hospital, followed by rehabilitation. Despite the fact that he still had some facial scars and a decided limp, he persuaded the Army not to discharge him. Instead, they transferred him from the Infantry to the Quartermaster Corps to teach courses involving combat.

Welsh didn't have time (or didn't *take* time) to orient Captain Rucker, who probably would have refused to be oriented, so Rucker knew nothing about the operations of the 114th. What I was unaware of was the overall plan. The 114th was to merge with the 973rd Graves Registration Company attached to the Eighth Army headquartered in Seoul. Captain Rucker was to take command of the combined unit. I was to take over the UNMC (United Nations Military Cemetery) and my S&R (Search & Recovery) platoon was to leave Masan and relocate in Wonju to search for the more recent MIAs in and around the battle areas of the Punch Bowl and the Iron Triangle, with names like "Old Baldy," "White Horse," "Jackson Heights," "T-Bone," and "Pork Chop." The plan made sense, but it really upset me. I wanted to continue leading the S&R effort and dreaded the thought of taking over the cemetery.

I spent those next weeks in Masan, at least every spare opportunity I had, going out with Kim into the countryside. We'd stop in villages and talk to the village masters in hopes of making a recovery similar to the one we made near the Hapch'an ferry crossing. I was still hopeful of finding Jacques L'Blanc, the MIA from New Iberia, LA.

One possibility was, of course, that Jacques L'Blanc (as well as others reported as MIA) had been captured and was a POW—that is, if he survived. About 8,000 U.S. GIs and 1,000 British were captured, most of them during the first six months of the war. About half of them died in captivity. The North Koreans were rough on them and subjected them to brainwashing, in hopes of converting them to communistic ideology. The media devoted plenty of coverage about the 22 (one Brit) "turncoats" who refused to be a part of the prisoner swap and elected to remain in North Korea.

◆   ◆   ◆

Of interest to me—for whatever reason—it was now time to harvest the rice. The mothers and daughters were prominent during the planting season, but the farmers and their sons did the harvesting. First they went out into the paddies, which were then dry, with machete-looking knives and cut the stalks. Then they gathered and tied the stalks into bundles and carried the bundles or loaded them onto donkeys or ox-driven carts to an area suited for the harvest process. They removed the long, silky pods, which contained the rice kernels, and piled them onto large straw mats. They saved the leafy stalks to use as straw for rugs and basket-making and to make or reinforce the thatched roofs of their homes. Then the sons took turns taking an ingenious homemade thrasher and beating the pile of pods over and over again to separate the kernels of rice from the chaff. When they were satisfied and the wind was right, the farmer and three boys would each hold onto a corner of the mat and toss the mat upward so the wind would blow the chaff away, leaving the rice to come down upon the mat. They did this over and over again until they had a mound of rice kernels on the mat. After they removed and saved that batch of kernels they would repeat the whole process until the entire crop had been harvested.

One of my special enjoyments was getting a haircut. The Korean barbers and their female assistants were great. While the barber was cutting hair, one assistant would shine your boots and belt buckle while the other would give you a manicure. When the barber finished cutting hair, the chair was put in a full reclining position and the massaging began. The barber did shoulders, neck and scalp. The assistants did arms and legs.—Ahhhhh!

One of my special dislikes was the flies. I never liked flies; I was taught that they carried germs. New Orleans had its share, as did every other place I had been. But Korea had more flies than one can possibly imagine, and it was always on my mind that they swarmed on and around the Honey Buckets and Honey Wagons and the fertilizer in the rice paddies. Aggressive, annoying flies were everywhere, year round. I had a good fly swatter. When I was at my desk I swatted and piled them up to make a new pyramid every day, but the fly population seemed to remain constant. I swatted in my room until it was fly-free, thanks to the mosquito netting.

Without Harry there was only one person at the Top of the Mark I could just sit and talk to: Captain Clark, the Protestant chaplain. He and I traded information on places of interest in the region around Masan. I took him with me to the 2nd Marine Division to see one of their USO shows. He took me to a magnificent Buddhist Temple and to the orphanage in which he involved himself with so much dedicated compassion.

One day, out of curiosity, I decided to go to Auction Day at the salvage yards. When I got there they were auctioning combat boots. There was a mountain high pile of boots. The auctioneer yelled out to the bidders, "Base your bids on five thousand pair—guaranteed, guaranteed, guaranteed!!!" Then he began his chant—not a word of it did I understand—until all of a sudden he declared, "SOLD!" Then he, followed by the crowd, went over to the pile of steel helmets, then to canteens and so forth until all of the piles were sold.

One of the active bidders struck up a conversation with me. His name was something like Max Yunklevich. He was the one that bought the combat boots. I happened to be standing next to him when he missed out on the battle fatigues. He seemed to be bound and determined to buy that enormous pile. The bidding was going so fast that it was difficult for me to keep up. The bidders lifted a finger or their eyebrows and the auctioneer understood their bid. My man quit just when I thought he was the winner. He was a short fat man with bushy, salt and peppery hair. His eyeglasses were very thick and he began to stare at me. Then, in a very thick Eastern European accent, he asked, "Yura yid?"

I answered, "I'm Jewish, yes."

He asked, "Vashtesh Yiddish?"

I replied, "Very, very little." I knew that *vashtesh* meant, "Do you understand?"

Growing up, I had some exposure to Yiddish, but never picked it up, other than a few words and expressions, most, I guess, from the many Yiddish-oriented jokes we all heard. My father's parents, Abraham and Adele, with whom I spent quite a lot of time—especially on holidays like Passover Seder and Christmas Eve—yes, Christmas with the decorated tree, stockings hanging from the fireplace, the works. We even painted eggs and had an Easter egg hunt on their front lawn. They spoke English to my brother and me, but when they spoke to each other they spoke a mixture of Yiddish and French. Most of my grandparents' family was in the perfume business, but my grandfather was a cap manufacturer. My Dad, who by the way had four brothers and eight sisters, was pretty fluent in Yiddish. He had picked up some from his parents, but most of what he knew came from the jewelry and diamond salesmen with whom he dealt. Whenever possible, he wanted me at his side when he did his buying. It was his way of getting me interested in and teaching me the business, but I never picked up on the Yiddish.

Max surprised me by inviting me to go with him to his ship. Out of curiosity, I accepted his invitation. He, the ship's captain, and I watched as the boots were loaded down into the hole of the ship. I asked the captain about a strange looking ship that looked like it was permanently anchored in the harbor. He explained that it was a power generating ship that provided electricity for the Masan area. Then we went into the lounge for drinks and dinner. Max loaded the automatic-changing turntable of his record player with a stack of 45 rpm records—all opera and classical music. He sang along with the opera and hummed or whistled along with the concertos and symphonies. When he was changing stacks of records he told me he was going to take the boots to Taiwan, where he could get them restored for practically nothing. Then he would take them to the States and sell them to Army-Navy Salvage stores. I invited Max to have dinner with me at the Top of the Mark, but he said he'd be leaving later that night. I gave him my address so he could let me know when he was going to return.

◆   ◆   ◆

Listening to Max's records stimulated lots of pleasant, musical memories. Max seemed pleased that I recognized many of the selections. I had taken Music Appreciation as one of my required elective courses at Newman School and had a part in the school production of "The Mikado." Music had always played an influential part of my life. My earliest memory was attending Mrs. Neason's dance school. I was three or four years old when I started. We were living in a one-bedroom apartment on the corner of Fourth and Camp in the Garden District of New Orleans. Mrs. Neason lived across the street and had her dance school in the garage. After my brother was born, in 1933, we moved to a two bedroom lower duplex on Roman Street near Napoleon Avenue. I attended Wilson Elementary School. We had assembly every morning. When the announcements were over we sang patriotic songs, Christmas carols, and recited The Lord's Prayer. Those of us who were learning to play musical instruments took turns entertaining. I took piano and clarinet lessons; others played the violin, trumpet, harmonica, and even the accordion. I did not like the music at Beth Israel Synagogue because I did not like the Cantor. He taught Hebrew. He was very strict and always had a ruler in his hand to slap us students whenever he felt it necessary. Anyway, at that time Hebrew was not a spoken language. All I was interested in was learning what was necessary for my Bar Mitzvah. The music at Sunday school wasn't too bad. I liked the songs associated with the holidays—Passover, Chanukah, Purim—as well as the prayers that were sung before drinking wine and eating bread. I was particularly drawn to the popular music we listened to on the radio—the big bands like Glenn Miller, Tommy Dorsey, Kaye Kaiser and a host of others, and the vocalists like Frank Sinatra, Peggy Lee, Dinah Shore and Louie Armstrong. All of us kept up with "The Hit Parade," a weekly radio program. It played the top ten hits of the week—in reverse order. We stayed glued to the end to hear the number one song of the week—to find out if our personal favorite had won. My Sunday school teacher was Victor Kirschman. He also drove the carpool in his 1939 yellow Buick convertible. He and his girlfriend wrote a song that made "The Hit Parade": "A kiss Good-night is all right/ But—re-mem-ber this/That A—Kiss Good-night leads to another kiss…"etc. Victor sang it so many times working out the lyrics that I felt like part of its creation. As far as opera, I didn't relate, except for some of the arias, especially in Puccini's *La'Bohem.* But I really liked the Gilbert and Sullivan operettas that we performed at Newman School. My very favorite, however, would have to be the music of Broadway. There was simply no music more enjoyable for me to get to know and enjoy.

◆   ◆   ◆

There were two projects I vowed to myself I would tackle during those times while I was in my office waiting for all of the S & R Teams to return. I wanted to learn how to type and I wanted to read the New Testament. Dick Priest worked with me on my typing and I practiced on my own. I did not do well.

I tried my very best to read the New Testament. I found it very difficult reading. Similar to my lack of belief that God wrote each and every word of the Old Testament, and thus infallible, I simply didn't believe the New Testament reflected the exact words of Jesus—"the one and only son of God"—and that it was thus infallible. How could they be *the* exact words of Jesus when the writings of the disciples contained inconsistencies on what the words were? But the inconsistencies are understandable because of the lapse of many years between the events and the writings by the disciples. I did notice, however, that many of teachings of Jesus reflected values expressed in the Old Testament, like "love your neighbor as yourself" and helping the poor, the sick and down trodden. I was appalled by the passages that condemned all future generations of Jews for the crucifixion of Jesus, in which they (and we) had no involvement. It seemed obvious to me that the early followers of Jesus were in competition with the Jewish establishment from which they broke away—that some of the written accounts were exaggerated and perhaps self-serving. They impressed me as being emotionally upset and determined to discredit—maybe even destroy—Judaism. My thought was that those anti-Jewish passages in the New Testament provided fodder to many ill-intentioned despots throughout history (the Inquisition, the pogroms, the confiscations, the expulsions, the humiliations, the Holocaust, all of the merciless torturing and slaughtering throughout he centuries). However, I did not have the nerve to share all of my thoughts with my friend Captain Clark, the Protestant chaplain—only the matter of the lapse of time between the events and the writings.

◆   ◆   ◆

I received cold, written orders from Captain Rucker, which really depressed me. The orders were for me to immediately send Sergeant O'Brien, Pfc. Casey and the S&R Platoon to Wonju. My clerk, Pfc. Priest, and I were to return to the 114th HQ in Pusan as soon as possible…

8

Life at the UNMC

Captain Rucker was all packed and ready to leave when Dick Priest and I drove through the front gate of the 114th HQ compound at the UNMC (United Nations Military Cemetery). Rucker seemed annoyed that it took us *that long* to drive a *measly* 50 miles. He had made arrangements with an Air Force friend of his stationed at K-9 to fly him to K-1, known as Kimpo, the U. S. Air Force HQ near Seoul. From there he said he was going to join the 114th Search and Recovery Platoon at Wonju. "You're in command here during my absence, Lieutenant. I expect daily reports," he said with a smirk as his driver sped him away.

Kim, the officer's house boy (not my little friend in Masan), carried all my things into the BOQ (Bachelor's Officers Quarters). Together, we unpacked and arranged my room. Then I walked over to the HQ quonset and talked to First Sergeant John McKillen, the top NCO (non-commissioned officer) of the Company. He was a career army man who had served in World War II. He thrived on military life and was a creature of the system. He had the company well-trained to all the daily routines: reveille at daybreak, inspection at parade ground formation, followed by announcements and the daily dozen exercises, retreat at sundown, and taps at curfew. Every Monday morning he conducted a very strict ritual. "Hit the deck for 'Pecker Check'" he would yell out as he entered the enlisted men's barracks right after reveille when the men first awoke. "Pecker check" was a visual inspection for venereal disease. Gonorrhea (the "clap"), was the most common of the diseases and there was plenty of it. If contracted, the infection could be discovered by a simple test the Monday morning after a GI returned from a weekend pass. If there were symptoms, the medics gave him a series of penicillin shots. There were other more serious venereal diseases; for some there was no easy cure, for others, no cure at all.

Figure 30—THP's houseboy, Kim, at BOQ

Sgt. McKillen was particularly strict when it came to sentry and guard duties. We needed extra good security. Our compound was an attractive target for thieves because of the many valuable personal effects of the deceased.

Lt. Dortch was on temporary assignment at KComZ (Korean Communication Zone) QM headquarters in Teagu. All of this meant that as the only commissioned officer I would be the OD (Officer of the Day) *every* day. As OD, I would witness every "pecker check," inspect the men in formation every morning, be responsible for signing every report and written order, be present at every retreat ceremony, and make unannounced inspections of the sentries and guards at odd times during the night. Every Friday afternoon it would be my responsibility to lecture the men on VD and dope—the two major hazards of going out on weekend pass. The lecture included ways to minimize the chances of contracting venereal disease and ways to avoid even experimenting with dope. I made the men aware that the prostitutes would push dope on them—even inoculate them while they slept (or after they passed out)—in hopes of getting them hooked. I had all of that in addition to my primary responsibilities as Chief Administrative Officer, Mortuary Officer, and Cemetery Officer of the UNMC.

Sgt. McKillen and I worked assignments and schedules out for the coming week, Then I returned to the BOQ, drank a beer and smoked a cigarette.

Captain Rucker, realizing I would soon arrive at the 114th HQ, had ordered all my mail set aside there rather than forwarded to Masan. I had a pile of mail and a lot of packages. Louise and all the other members of my family, plus some friends, had sent a variety of presents for our third wedding anniversary and for my 24th birthday. Louise sent me a subscription to the international edition of

The Wall Street Journal. This was a special weekly edition printed on lightweight onion skin paper. For my birthday she sent an extensive selection of hors d'oeuvres and specialty foods from Zager's Delicatessen. Those were things I genuinely could use at cocktail hour. Now all I needed were some fellow officers with whom to share the treasures.

Sgt. McKillen had made a special point of inviting me to the NCO Club on entertainment night, But in my position, I knew I'd be better off maintaining a distance by not fraternizing with the NCOs and enlisted men. It would be different if I had another officer to go with. The way things were arranged, my meals would be served at the officers' table in the mess hall. In addition to separate living quarters, I had separate bath and washroom facilities. The wash facility was inside the BOQ. Someone had constructed (improvised) it by recessing two steel helmets into cut-outs in a wooden "counter top." The helmets were removable. It was Kim's job to keep clean hot water in one and cold water in the other. That's where I washed-up, brushed my teeth and shaved.

There was another reason I avoided being around these enlisted men as much as possible. They were different than those in my S&R Platoon, most of whom had college educations; some even had graduate school degrees. Here the average education was fifth or sixth grade. Here they were mostly draftees from rural areas or inner city slums and fit for not much more than common labor. There was a problem of communication and understanding. In every sentence it was f**k'n this or muddaf**k'r that, or, "Oz needs t'git t'da'pom-pom hoochie, L'tenant. Oz jes gots t'git ma p***y, or ah gits a muddaf**k'n headache."

There were exceptions, of course, and those got the better jobs. My favorite, in addition to Dick Priest, was a very likable Private First Class (PFC) named Lionel. He was an excellent clerk-typist. His desk was next to mine and he would go out of his way to be helpful. I could carry on a decent conversation with him without each sentence being laced with cuss words. Growing up, I never heard my father use a cuss word. My mother had her favorite, but the only time I ever heard her use it was when she burned her finger while cooking or similar incidents. During officers' training they emphasized that people who constantly use cuss words show an inability to express themselves in clear, understandable English; therefore, they urged commissioned officers not to use them.

My official office was located in the Administration Quonset up near the entrance to the Cemetery and across from the Mortuary. My desk was one of five in the large front room. The sergeant who was my assistant at the UNMC and four clerk-typists occupied the other four desks. One wall was lined with cabinets which contained the tens of thousands of files of all those who had been processed through the UNMC since the UNMC first came into existence in 1950. The next room contained all of the radio equipment. That's where Dick Priest spent the day. The supply room was in the very rear, and it needed a good cleaning out.

"Good morning, *rutenant*; I am Captain Yon, your interpreter." Despite being a captain in the ROK Army, Captain Yon was a very shy little man. He projected no military presence in his thick eyeglass lenses and his baggy pants. Actually, he was a chemist who had managed to escape from the North. His family had owned a successful nail and screw manufacturing business. When the Communists took over after World War II, they confiscated the factory and killed all of his family. At the time, he was at the University of Seoul getting an advanced degree in Chemistry and Metallurgy, which saved his life. His main function at the 114th was interpreting the daily, on-going communications between Mr. Lee, the foreman, and me. Mr. Lee (not my interpreter in Masan) was the head supervisor over all the Korean laborers that we used to maintain the grounds and handle the deceased. Captain Yon did very well for himself on his time off. He somehow acquired liquids containing silver, like silver nitrate solution, and in his home lab he would extract the silver from the solution. Then he would sell the silver nuggets, for which there was a huge demand because most of the women's adornments were made out of silver.

Figure 31—Captain Yon

◆   ◆   ◆

It did not take long for news to get around that there was a new Cemetery officer at the UNMC. Liaisons from the various participating forces began to call or visit. I heard first from the British. They were so proper. A courier delivered a written invitation for me to join them at their HQ for dinner. I accepted, also by courier. When I arrived at the British HQ I was ushered into the officers' lounge. It was simply furnished, but functional. The commander introduced me to the four members of his staff while cocktails were served. I ordered scotch. The drinks were hearty, but with only one small ice cube. After a couple of double-shot drinks we entered the dining room and were formally served several courses, with a different kind of wine with each course. The main entrée was lamb—two tiny chops each. (Queen Elizabeth had declared a period of austerity and the British everywhere, even the armed forces in Korea, honored it.) With the lamb, they served bland little new potatoes, carrots and peas. Dessert consisted of very sharp cheese and crackers, served with port wine. After dessert we returned to the lounge, where they served demitasse, and we smoked, pipes, cigars and cigarettes, which filled the lounge with smoke and rich aroma.

The conversation then turned to the various ceremonies the British planned to conduct at the UNMC. Each battalion had its traditions—some dated back hundreds of years. Tradition dictated that they conduct very formal ceremonies at the UNMC, both when a battalion arrived and when it departed Korea.

Only the British invited me for dinner. The other participating forces sent their liaisons. Some, like the Ethiopians and the Greeks, brought presents. The Commanding General of the French force came by, but he only seemed interested in having his picture taken while placing a bouquet of flowers at the base of the flag in front of the French section.

The liaison from the Netherlands came to my office unannounced. The Dutch captain spoke in a loud, hurried manner, right up in my face. His voice was so loud that Dick Priest came from the radio room to see what was happening. When I started wiping the spit off of my face and out of my eyes, Dick, Lionel and the other clerks couldn't hold back their laughter.

Liaisons from the Canadian and Thai forces came by to plan ceremonies. The Thai liaison was cooperative and appreciative, but the Canadian liaison was demanding and difficult.

Figure 32—Thai Liaison

◆   ◆   ◆

There was a steady stream of visitors to the UNMC, especially on weekends. We tried to guide them by means of strategically placed signs. We had our own sign-making capability. One of the persistent problems was dealing with curiosity seekers. They kept getting into the mortuary, despite the fact that we had a very prominent sign that read "AUTHORIZED PERSONNEL ONLY."

We tried different wording and locations. They continued to ignore our signs. As an experiment, I had the sign maker make a discrete little sign that read, "Mortuary personnel *must* remove gloves before touching door knobs." It worked! No more curiosity seekers. However, I never did find an effective way to prevent people from taking pictures of individual graves or the graves of the Russian pilots. I did, though, remove a sign near the entrance. The sign read, "We'll be the last ones to let you down."

◆   ◆   ◆

The High Holy Days came early. There were two locations in Korea where services were to be held: Seoul and Pusan. Harry Martin, my quonset-mate in Masan, called from Teague to say he would be coming to Pusan for services and would stay with me. Also, my friend Joe Bernstein called to say he was planning to come down to attend Yom Kippur services with me. Joe, too, was sidetracked on his way to Korea to attend the CBR Warfare School in Eta Jima. At that time he was assigned as Operational Officer of the Petroleum Depot in Yong Dong Po near Seoul. It turned out to be a real warm get-together with all of the 'Bama' graduates from the QM Supply Depot and all of the visitors. The services themselves were overcrowded with servicemen, DOD civilians, and medical corps doctors and nurses. Rabbi Estersohn had his hands full leading the services for such a huge congregation, consisting of all branches of Judaism. During most of the service there was lots of confusion—GI's going in and out—everybody on a different page. However, when we all recited the *Shama* (the holiest prayer in Jewish liturgy) it sounded like one voice. A lump formed in my throat and an indescribable feeling of deep emotion engulfed me. I was not the only one who felt the spirituality of that moment, in that setting. It was awesome.

◆   ◆   ◆

My first major VIP visit was by a group of U.S. Senators and Representatives led by Senator William Knowland, the Senate majority leader; and of course Ambassador Briggs, the U.S. Ambassador to Korea; a couple of generals and their entourage. Senator Knowland had been very instrumental in drafting the United Nations Charter and was very well-known and respected. There were quite a number of newspaper reporters and cameramen in the entourage. After the tour they strolled around the main area. Each participating country in the UN effort had a square section of 100 grave sites with its flag front and center. A Congressman approached me and in a low voice asked, "Whose flag is that over there, Lieutenant, with only two graves in the section?" In a low voice I replied, "That is the flag of India, which only has an ambulance unit in Korea. Unfortunately, the ambulance ran off the road and down a steep embankment." Then the Congressman confessed he was unaware that India was a participant in the war and he could not remember ever having seen the flag of India before. It had only been about six years since India had gained its independence from the British.

Afterwards they settled into a picture-taking session. They included me in some of the pictures, but I never did know if any of them got into print.

◆   ◆   ◆

The Commanding General of the 32nd QM Group called a meeting of all company commanders in the Group. The only item on the agenda of interest to me was the football league. They wanted every company to participate. I was excited about organizing our team, conducting tryouts, and beginning practice sessions. It was a terrific boost to morale at the 114th.

Football was my favorite sport. Truthfully, it was about the only sport I was in fact good at. I was okay at tennis for someone without formal training (I had a great serve) and I played volleyball well—made first teams at ZBT at Alabama and at Fort Lee, VA (we played and beat West Point). However, I had above average coaching at football, plus I seemed to have a special talent for handling and passing the ball.

My Uncle Abie moved in with us after his discharge from the Army in 1944. He was an excellent athlete—an especially good softball pitcher. He would take me outside and throw every kind of ball with me for hours. He could tell that my strength was throwing overhand, rather than underhand so he concentrated on baseball and football, rather than softball. He had me throwing the football 45 and 50 yards and he improved my accuracy by hanging a rubber tire from a tree limb in the back yard so I could practice when he wasn't there. There was a vacant lot across the street where he coached me in passing to a moving receiver.

When I went out for the football team at Newman School, head coach Mr. Harris and his assistant "Chick" Henson were impressed with my passing ability. Unfortunately, they used the single wing formation, which was best suited for a running game. Some college teams were in the early stages of adopting the "T" formation, but it had not yet reached the high school level. Despite that, Coach Harris made it his business to learn how to coach the "T" formation. He also added some new passing plays out of the single wing.

In my senior year I did very well. My name was in the paper after (almost) every game, especially after our Homecoming Game against Rugby Academy. (Rugby Academy was one of the all-boys military high schools in New Orleans.) The game was scoreless, with only a few minutes to play. Rugby was moving the ball well toward our goal. I was playing defensive secondary behind the line backers. Rugby called a pass play and I covered a receiver heading toward the sideline to my right. The pass was short and easy for me to intercept. From there it was a wide open field for me to run the 70 or so yards for a Newman touchdown. We won, six to nothing!

ZBT, the popular Jewish fraternity at Tulane, literally recruited me. They had me working out with their football team even before rush season began. During that first year at Tulane, the Zebe's at Alabama started urging me to transfer to Tuscaloosa. I did transfer after my freshman year, not for football reasons, but because I wanted more of a college experience. Attending Tulane was not much different to me than high school at Newman When I got to Alabama I considered going out for the Varsity football team as a walk-on, but at 5'11", 172 lbs., and not being a speed demon, after watching one practice session I quickly decided it wasn't a good idea. I did enjoy playing quarterback for ZBT in the fraternity league the next three years until I graduated.

Lucky for me, the Army played under the same rules as the college fraternities: two-handed touch. Having had four years of fraternity experience, I was the logical coach, quarterback, and tail back for the 114th "Diggers." I was able to utilize the same playbook, pass patterns and defenses to which I was so familiar.

The season went very well. We only lost one game, and that was to a team that went undefeated. In touchdown passes I was ranked second, with eight. The winner was a college quarterback who got drafted. He threw 21, won our league, and went on to win the KCOMZ but lost in the finals to the Eighth Army champions.

My biggest problem was the playing field. There were several marked off on the parade grounds. There was little, if any grass—mostly gravel. Two-handed touch is a rough game. It's fast, hard hitting, and you do not wear any padding. (At 'Bama' my left shoulder was dislocated on two different occasions.) Each time I went sprawling on that gravel surface I got skinned; by the end of the game my knees and elbows were a bloody mess.

The medics did what they could to get me ready for the next game. I had my choice between Mercurochrome and Methiolate. The first was bright red; it didn't sting when applied, but neither did it do much good as far as healing was concerned. The second was light orange in color; when applied it stung unmercifully, but it helped the healing.

The other pastimes that helped were first and foremost the mail, both receiving and writing it. Delivery continued to be irregular and undependable. It definitely affected my mood, whether I received mail or not. Louise kept me up-to-date on what was going on at her job, as well as all the Southern gossip. She was asked to be a bride's maid in Jackie Diamond's wedding, and that was a big happy event. She would ask me to see if I could find interesting gifts for certain occasions, such as her Aunt Jeanne and Joe Rosenberg's anniversary. I wrote about the events of my day, and I did things like ask Louise to send some winter clothes and English primers for Kim, my little friend.

I did quite a bit of reading. When I left home I packed *The Caine Mutiny* and *Beau Geste*. I thoroughly enjoyed both of those. Then I started reading Mickey Spillane thrillers and kept up with the adventures of Mike Hamner.

There was a movie almost every night. The movies were old and we had seen most of them back in the States, but it was a way of relaxing.

Occasionally there was a USO Show; they were entertaining and a good divergence—a boost to morale.

The radio helped a lot. I had bought a good short wave, had it next to my bed, and when I found a clear station somewhere playing contemporary hit records like Joni James singing "Ruby," I'd just leave it on all night. The Australian stations were easy to pick up clearly and were fun to listen to. Then, of course, there was always the United States Armed Forces Radio, which attempted to pep us up, as opposed to Radio Moscow, which tried to demoralize us.

◆   ◆   ◆

Our mortuary operations were at full strength, despite the cease-fire. There was a continuous flow of "currents"—victims of vehicle and miscellaneous accidents, homicides, land mines, natural causes and guerrilla activities. (The NKPA and the Chinese were especially good at infiltrating our lines and wreaking havoc. They would get through our check points by dressing as little old women and tricks like that.) We received a bird colonel that choked to death on a pork chop bone. Our Search and Recovery platoon was sending us a large number of MIA recoveries from the recent battle sights. We processed all of those remains, and then escorted them to the CIU in Kokura, Japan, for positive identification.

In addition, now that the fighting had ceased the UN gave each participating country the option of what to do with their deceased. Each country could have the remains disinterred and sent back home, which most elected to do; or they could leave them at the UNMC. The British had always adhered to the policy of "where the tree falls, let it lie." The French let each family decide for themselves; furthermore, each family could change its mind at any time.

Just this part of our operation kept two clerk-typists and fifty laborers busy full time.

Lionel, my best clerk-typist, asked to escort a MIA to Kokura and take his five-day R & R there. I agreed, even though I didn't have a replacement that could do his work. He and his companion-for-the-week were biking out in the countryside on a bicycle built for two when the bike skidded off the road, down into a ravine, where Lionel's head hit a rock or a tree limb and fractured his skull. He never regained consciousness and passed away after a few days in a coma. The Army notified Lionel's parents with its usual form letter: "We regret to notify you of the death of your son, etc." It was my responsibility to explain the circumstances to Lionel's parents and sister. By letter I expressed my condolences, told how much I thought of him, and enclosed a copy of the report detailing the accident. I described the memorial service we conducted in our chapel and repeated some of the dear words spoken by his close friends. I omitted a part of the prayer that his closest friend delivered. He prayed that Lionel had finally lost his virginity before the accident.

Figure 33—Chapel at the UNMC

That wasn't the only letter I wrote to the next-of-kin. Frequently, I would receive letters as Cemetery Officer begging for information—any information—informing them what had happened to their loved one. In most cases I had little, if any, first hand knowledge of what had happened. All I could do was review the file and do the best I could to assure them that their loved one was treated with the highest level of reverence. Whenever there was a request in which I was personally involved in the recovery, I provided all the details I felt appropriate to provide and I did receive appreciative responses.

◆   ◆   ◆

Joe Bernstein and I were able to talk by telephone late in the evenings when the circuits were not quite so busy. We made plans for me to visit him in Yong Dong Po, near Seoul, after he got back from R&R in Japan, and subject to my being able to get Lt. Dortch to come down from KCOMZ HQ to cover for me. I was eager to see Seoul and the Eighth Army combat area. That gave me something exciting to anticipate…

9

Autumn in Pusan

The first day of October was a significant day for the Army in Korea. That's the day they finally turned on the heat and issued winter uniforms. There were days in September when we needed heat. The temperature dipped to freezing and there were many cold nights I could have used warmer clothes when I checked the guards, but it wasn't October One yet.

"Checking the guards," meant getting up out of a warm bed at least two random times during the night, getting dressed, and walking the perimeter of our compound. When a guard heard sounds of someone approaching, he would shout: "Halt!—Who goes there?" I would shout back: "Lt. Pailet, 02004577."

With his rifle at ready he would order "Advance and be recognized." With his flashlight shining directly in my face, I would obey and approach him and say the password of the day. We'd make small talk for awhile, and then I'd go on to the next guard post and so forth until I completed the rounds.

On one occasion I approached a guard who was sound asleep. That was an automatic court marshal; I had no alternative. Ordinarily, I let the sergeants handle the discipline problems so I could sit back and act as judge. The only other time I personally court-marshaled one of my men was when this foul-mouthed troublemaker refused to obey my direct order. I had ordered him to stop beating up another soldier half his size. He completely ignored me. It took four of us to pull him off of the poor victim and to restrain him until the MP's (Military Police) arrived.

At the Officers Training School at Fort Lee, VA, we were introduced to an Army axiom: six percent of the men in every outfit will be problematic. There were 100 men in the 114th HQ Compound. Therefore, according to the axiom, there would be six troublemakers. The axiom went on to say that if you got rid of one of those six, someone else in the unit would fill the void. It's evidently a psychological thing involving the need within some people to show off, to be the center of attraction, or just to be the one to disrupt. In Masan, with only 25 men, there was always one—usually one of the mechanics.

The remainder of the month of October and the early part of November was filled with activity: football games, VIP visits, planning and conducting ceremonies. The mortuary remained busy and the six percent rule proved itself. It was amazing how troublesome six men could be.

The weather began changing for the worse. One day it would be uncomfortably muggy, the next two days it would rain, Then the temperature would drop. Then the cycle would repeat itself, but each time it would get colder. Everybody, it seemed, was getting sore throats, headaches and fever. The infirmary was overflowing. As soon as I felt a scratchy throat I checked in with the medics. They gave me a large bottle of aspirin tablets and a quart jar of Codeine syrup. The combination worked pretty well. I kept a glass of Codeine-on-the-rocks near me at all times just to sip on when I felt the need.

Mail deliveries became somewhat more dependable. Louise wrote about her father's gout attacks, as well as the honors he was receiving from the Home Builders Association. She told me about the great money-saving buys she was getting on her clothes at work. She also wrote that she had been selected to take part in the Country Club's "Droopy Drawers" production. That was a satirical, meant-to-be-funny musical production, written, directed and performed (and made fun of) by members of the club. The show was presented every Thanksgiving. Louise was taking part in a hula-hula dance scene with grass skirts and lots of belly wiggle. They were already in rehearsal. She invited my brother Lester to come up from New Orleans for the occasion. He did, and had a great time.

I received a real long letter from my cousin Sidney (his mother was a Pailet). He was so happy! A few years earlier he and his sweetheart of the moment had married. The marriage quickly failed and ended in divorced. Sidney's father was a very successful businessman (owning a chain of retail shoe stores) and there was substantial alimony. Well, the big news was that she had remarried, which relieved Sidney of the alimony payments.

Sidney also filled me in on the New Orleans gossip. He brought me up-to-date on what was happening with the other members of our little high school clique. In addition to Sidney and me there were Danny Buckman, Louis Shushan, and Joe Bernstein, even though Joe was a year younger. We were wild teenagers during a wild time in New Orleans (which, by-the-way was pronounced "N'Awlins" by the natives). World War ll was still raging when we were 14 and 15. The two years following were just as wild. New Orleans was overloaded with fun-seeking service men, and the city looked the other way while the honky tonks catered to every vice. Despite the fact that he wasn't old enough to have a driver's license, Louis had the use of a car—a big navy blue '39 Buick Roadmaster. On weekends he would pick us up and we'd go down to the French Quarter and intermingle with the sailors and soldiers that were out on weekend passes. The influence was terrible, but we thought we were big stuff. Louis's father was part of Governor Huey P. Long's inner circle. He and others benefited immensely in terms of political favors. The only problem was the recipients of those favors didn't report to the IRS all they received as income. While Mr. Shushan and his cohorts were serving their time in the Federal Penitentiary, Louis's mother died. His father hired a housekeeper, cook, chauffeur and others to take care of Louis. When Mr. Shushan got "out," he leased two apartments for himself: one in the Roosevelt Hotel in New Orleans, the other in the Waldorf Astoria in New York City. So Louis sort of raised himself, living in the family home with servants on Versailles Place around the corner from our home on Audubon Blvd. I liked Louis and enjoyed the times we spent together. He had a brilliant mind and anything academically he attempted he did with ease and without flaw. I never knew him to make less than an A+ in any course.

Later, after each of us got a driver's license and use of a car, we intensified our wild escapades. During those years, in addition to the French Quarter, we went to the gambling houses, the racetrack and all sorts of smoke-filled nightclubs. The only vice I remember that we didn't at least *try* was dope. Along the riverfront there was a line of dingy dope dens. They were frequented by Merchant Marine sailors and weird-looking characters. We would walk by and look in, but I cannot remember any of us actually entering any of those dens.

We were less wild during the school week. During football season I was involved in afternoon practice. Danny and Sidney were on the basketball team and they had their afternoon practice.

◆   ◆   ◆

Albert Mintz was one of my earliest and best friends. Albert and I grew up together and were very close. We spent a lot of time together during the years we were preparing to become Bar Mitzvah and continuing our Jewish education until Confirmation. The night of Confirmation, following the afternoon service, the entire class—all eight of us—celebrated by going to the Blue Room of the Roosevelt Hotel. That was one of the famous supper clubs in the country. (Some others were the Stork Club in New York, the Pump Room in Chicago and the Peabody Hotel in Memphis). These clubs featured a live stage show, great food, and a sophisticated ambiance. They served as a showcase for the big bands: Glenn Miller, Tommy Dorsey, Benny Goodman, and great instrumentalists like Buddy Rich or Gene Kruper on the drums, Harry James on the trumpet, and Lionel Hampton on the xylophone. Frank Sinatra, Ella Fitzgerald and Louie Armstrong, among others, appeared with other great artists. They rotated in and out about every two weeks. All of these performances were broadcast live on clear-channel radio around the country to loyal and enthusiastic listeners.

Albert was an A-level tennis player and unbeatable at ping pong. However, he was only a peripheral member of our clique. The reason? Albert was a dedicated student with a driving ambition to become a doctor or a lawyer as soon as possible. He was a zealous student. At Newman School he added extra courses, skipped grades, and graduated early. He breezed through Tulane undergraduate and entered law school while I was having fun partying and taking it easy at Alabama.

Another after-school activity we enjoyed when we got the chance was to go over to the home of one of the girls who was in our circle of friends. There were three that invited friends over to listen to records and learn the latest dance steps: Audrey Burka, Joan Friedler, and Marie Louise Levy. They had great record collections: Dinah Shore, Vaughn Monroe, Peggy Lee, the Big Bands, and always the top ten on the Hit Parade. They knew all the new jitterbug, rumba and slow dance steps and served refreshments. It was a fun way to spend some time before going home to do our homework.

The girls had a way of titillating the boy they were dancing with, especially when they were slow dancing to songs like "Far Away Places" by Perry Como. Well, when Sidney asked the girl he had a crush on to teach him how to slow dance, that's when they began a relationship that quickly escalated. It went from a kiss goodnight to necking, to petting, to "everything but," to engagement, to marriage. We had no reliable birth control methods and we understood the social consequences of premarital intercourse. If an unmarried girl got pregnant and the boy refused to marry her, she would drop out of school and disappear, rather than face the disgrace. Her parents would send her off some place to have the baby. After she gave birth, she would either return to a different school or the whole family would leave town. The girls' mothers had taught their daughters the dangers (some instilled so much fear in their daughters they became frigid and incapable of ever thawing out), but at the same time they encouraged their daughters to find a nice (rich) Jewish boy and raise a family.

Boys' parents rarely taught their sons about sex. At the most they made remarks like, "You get that girl pregnant and you know you'll have to marry her.

Then you'll have to give up your education and go out and get a job. You're much too young to be thinking about marriage. You'll meet many girls before you're ready to settle down."

During high school I had crushes from time to time on one girl or the other, but the crushes never lasted very long. I never "went" with a girl until my freshman year at Tulane. ZBT pledges were required to bring a Jewish date to all of the fraternity's social functions. The upper classmen snapped up all of the incoming freshmen girls, which made it very hard for us freshmen to find a date. Lucky for me, I met a very nice Jewish girl one day quite by accident. She was a senior at McMain, the large girls' public high school. (None of the public or Catholic high schools in New Orleans were co-ed. Newman school was co-ed, and so were most of the other private schools, except for the military academies). I asked her if she would go with me to a ZBT party. She was thrilled to be able to go to a Tulane fraternity party. It worked well for both of us, so for the rest of the year the two of us went to all of the parties and other events where dates were required.

◆   ◆   ◆

On a beautiful, crisp day toward the end of October, the highest-ranking officers in the U.S. Army were in the Pusan area. Luckily, we were alerted that the UNMC was on the list of likely places these VIPs might inspect. The alert gave us the time we needed to clean up, dress-up, and have everything looking its very best because we had no idea what they would ask to see if they came. Lo and behold, the UNMC was the first place they decided to visit. A caravan of 17 limousines drove through our front gates, down the long driveway, and wound its way to the cemetery. I was waiting at the entrance all pressed and polished (thanks to Kim, my houseboy), with my ascot and swagger stick. I took an extra deep swallow when I saw four stars on the flags of the first three limousines. The lead limo came to a stop right in front of me. PFC Priest, who was wearing a bright, white enameled steel helmet and white gloves, stepped forward and opened the rear door of the first limo. The Chief of Staff of the U.S. Army, General Matthew Ridgeway, stepped out. I snapped to attention, gave him my best salute, and nervously shouted out, "Lt. Theodore H. Pailet reporting, *sir*."

Figure 34—Pfc. Priest, Gen Ridgeway, THP, Gen Hull & Gen Maxwell
Taylor

The general returned my salute, then extended his hand to shake mine, and in a calm voice said, "At ease, Lieutenant." While all the other VIPs were getting out of the limos, the general asked me if I would lead the way. Of course I agreed. Before we left on the tour, he introduced me to the other four-star generals: General Hull, head of the Far East Command, General Maxwell Taylor, Eighth Army Commander, and several lower ranking generals in his entourage.

General Ridgeway had been a no-nonsense commander of the 82nd Airborne Division during World War II. During the first year of the Korean War, when General Walker was killed in a jeep accident, General MacArthur selected Matthew Ridgeway as the overall commander of the UN Forces in Korea. When President Truman fired General MacArthur, the president appointed Ridgeway to succeed MacArthur as the Far East Commander in Tokyo. From there, Ridgeway went on to the Pentagon.

There were a large number of three, two and one star generals, field grade officers, some Department of the Army civilians, and a few congressmen. Tours such as this were conducted according to the strict rules of military protocol—that is, by rank. Since I was conducting the tour and since we would form a column two abreast, I was at the front, to the left of the ranking officer: General Ridgeway. Next were Generals Hull and Taylor; the others followed. It seemed as if they were strung out a mile long. First, I led them toward the mortuary, close enough so they could see a stack of recovered MIAs we had recently received, and some newly arriving current deceased—the black body bags being unloaded from a six-by truck and being stacked up to await processing. This was also within view of the disinterment operation involving a number of Frenchmen in progress. I gave a brief explanation of each process.

Figure 35—Gen Ridgeway, THP, Gen Taylor

"General, would you like to inspect the inside of the mortuary?" I asked.

"No, Lieutenant, that won't be necessary," he answered. So I showed them the enemy section, then headed toward the main area of the UN cemetery, which was the most attractive with its manicured grounds and all the colorful flags waving in the breeze from the East Sea (a/k/a "The Sea of Japan" by the Japanese). On the way, the general said, "Lieutenant, you may not know this, but I dedicated this cemetery back in 1951. It was an awesome ceremony, very touching. Before this cemetery was established, we had five or six battlefield cemeteries located in areas near some of the heavy fighting. After we secured the south, it made more sense to consolidate everything here." I thanked the general for sharing that information with me.

Figure 36—Gen Hull, Gen Ridgeway, THP

When we got in front of the UN flag, Ridgeway laid a wreath and made some appropriate remarks. Newspaper reporters took copious notes, pictures were taken, and they all mulled around for a while, asked questions, and finally returned to their respective limos and drove off.

◆   ◆   ◆

From time to time I had visits from Harry Martin, Jim Timmerville, and from Kim. Jim Timmerville was a quonset-mate of ours in Masan and a great volley-ball player. Harry was still with KMAG. He was applying for early release. In order to qualify for early release you had to either be in the Eighth Army, having spent so many months in a front line combat assignment, or having been accepted into a graduate school in the States. The disadvantage of early release was that you had to extend your reserve commitment from two to four years. Harry was eager to study law, as well as to rotate home to his family and fiancé. He got accepted to Harvard Law School, which was an awesome accomplishment, and was certain to qualify for early release, but it took constant diligence on his part to make sure he was included.

Figure 37—THP, Harry Martin, Jim Timmerville, Capt. Lee

I seriously considered doing something similar, but at the time I didn't feel the urge to go back to school for another three years. I wanted to go into business. That's what I had studied. My father had a thriving jewelry business and Louise's dad had a successful land development and home-building business. Above all, I did not want to extend my reserve commitment for an additional two years. Trouble seemed to be brewing in Southeast Asia. Communist guerillas were giving the French a bad time in Viet Nam, Cambodia, and Laos. Viet Nam had been divided, North and South, at the end of World War II. The North was Communist, led by Ho Chi Min, and the South was a Colony of France. To me, it looked like a war was inevitable. I heard all of this on my short wave radio.

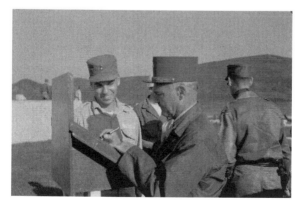

Figure 38—Commanding General of French Asian Forces

Kim, my little friend, was in lower school in Masan. Because of that he could only visit me in Pusan on the weekends when he could arrange a round-trip ride. I enjoyed his visits. He took an intense interest in whatever I was doing at work. After dinner we'd see whatever movie was showing or go to a USO show. Before bed I would read stories out loud and help him read English from the books that Louise sent to me for him.

◆   ◆   ◆

Joe Bernstein called me when he returned from R&R in Japan. He had a wonderful time, but it took a few days for him to recover. That was typical. We made arrangements for me to visit him in Yong Dong Po. To get to Yong Dong Po I had to take the train (there was only one). It left from Pusan about 8 o'clock in the evening, made one stop in Teagu, and arrived in Seoul early in the morning. There were a limited number of sleepers, so I scheduled my departure date the first time I could reserve a sleeper and arrange for Lt. Dortch to come down from Teagu to cover for me the few days I would be away.

Taking the train involved anxieties. The guerillas took great pleasure in taking pot shots at the train as it twisted and turned through the mountainous countryside. Sometimes they would sabotage the tracks and cause wrecks. These incidents slowed down somewhat after the cease-fire agreement, but they did not stop completely. Fortunately, my trip to Seoul went without incident and I got a good night's sleep.

Joe met me at the station and gave me a tour of downtown Seoul before driving over the Han River to Yong Dong Po. Downtown Seoul was a bombed-out disaster. Only the few buildings constructed of reinforced masonry had the resemblance of the former structure, and even those were gutted. Everything else was rubble.

Figure 39—THP in downtown Seoul

Joe's petroleum depot and living quarters were impressive, but nothing I had seen in Korea was as magnificent as the Officers' Club at Eighth Army Headquarters at Kimpo Air Force Base. We went there each night because the drinks, the food, the service and the atmosphere were number one.

Joe was able to take a full day off. We drove to the front lines to visit Mark Golden, one of our ZBT fraternity brothers at Tulane. Mark, a 1st Lieutenant assigned to the First Marine Division, commanded an amphibious assault platoon. His battalion was stationed along the 38th parallel—the truce line. The Han River separated his outfit from the Communist Chinese and North Koreans. The weather was bitter cold, with gusty Artic winds. Joe found Mark's HQ, drove up and approached the clerk on duty

"We are here to see Lt. Golden."

The clerk replied, "No telling where he is, sir. His BOQ is over yonder. If he's not there, you might look for him down at the river bank. He likes to hunt ducks down there."

That's where we found him. He and his friend were duck hunting on the south side of the river while some Red Chinese and NKPA officers were doing the same thing on the north side. When someone shot a duck, the duck belonged to the hunters on whatever side of the river the duck fell. Mark had about six ducks and needed just a few more for the officers in his outfit to have a duck dinner.

Mark was really surprised and pleased to see us. We visited for an hour or so. Before we left we took a few precious pictures, despite the bitter cold. (Not long after our visit, Mark was wounded during a mortar attack. He was air-lifted to a MASH unit and awarded a Purple Heart.)

Figure 40—Lt Mark Golden & Lt Joe Bernstein

◆   ◆   ◆

Dick Priest was waiting for me when I returned to the 114th. "Lieutenant, the hospital at the Depot has been calling for you. They won't tell me why. Here's the number and who to ask for." I finally got through to Major Something-or-other, the head of nursing. She pleaded for me to come as soon as possible. When I got there I was ushered into a private room (a rarity) and met an Army nurse, with her captain's bars pinned on the short hospital gown she was wearing—void of modesty. She was sitting on pillows in a large chair next to the bed. She was somewhat attractive, but she looked sad and upset—like she had been crying a lot. She had given birth to a stillborn baby. No, she didn't have any idea who the father was, because in her words she "just loved to make love." Two things were of utmost importance to her: that this matter be kept strictly confidential, and that her baby be buried in the UNMC. As soon as I gave those two assurances she seemed relieved, got up from the chair, and walked me all the way to my jeep.

◆   ◆   ◆

December was a busy month at the UNMC. It was marked by, among other things many ceremonies by Regiments or Battalions that were departing Korea in order to be home by Christmas. Some of the ceremonies were extraordinarily elaborate, especially England's First Kings Regiment, Scotland's Black Watch Battalion, and the Greek regiment. The First Kings is the city regiment of

Manchester and Liverpool; it was formed in 1685. Its motto is "Difficulties Be Damned." The Black Watch is actually the 42nd Royal Highland Regiment. It was formed in 1725 and was prominent in the defeat of Napoleon. These regiments, with their incredibly long and cherished traditions, conducted ceremonies that were unbelievably impressive. The ceremonies were solemnly choreographed and featured remarks by the commanding officer. These remarks went on for an hour or more, with the troops standing motionless at parade rest. Four honor guards, each at least six-foot six, stood at the corners of the podium…their rifles at parade rest, their heads in a respectful bow.

Figure 41—England's First Kings Regiment

Figure 42—Scotland's Black Watch Battalion

What made the Greek ceremony interesting was that it was in actual fact a religious service. The regimental chaplain wore his black robe and all his formal

vestments, and even though the ceremony was entirely in Greek you could tell
that the entire regiment was Greek Orthodox.

Figure 43—Greek Ceremony

Figure 44—Turkish Battalion Ceremony

◆   ◆   ◆

When time allowed, which was seldom, I went shopping for Christmas presents, which had to be mailed no later than the first week in December. We
played the last of our football games and I spent time hosting friends and guests.
The Replacement Center was right across the road from the UNMC, so I got to

see many of my friends (including Harry Martin) as they were being processed to rotate back to the States.

I was within 60 or 70 days of leaving myself. What had been no more than a fantasy was now becoming more palpable. Thoughts of being together with Louise, of going home to see my mother, dad and brother, of just returning to the good ole USA, injected excitement into each and every day.

The work load at the cemetery remained at a high pitch, even though, thankfully, the number of current deceased and the number of disinterments had begun to slacken. We were still busy with recoveries of MIAs and accident victims, and the number of inspections began to increase. It seemed that every participating nation found a reason to visit the UNMC, and now the United Nations began to conduct all sorts of inspections and investigations. The UN sent one team after another to look into matters that had been put on hold during the heavy fighting. The teams would interrogate me about a whole variety of subjects having to do with the work of the 114th. I never really knew exactly what they were looking for, and I never received any sort of report relating to their visit.

Figure 45—UN Inspection Team

At least it kept my mind occupied and helped make the time go by a little faster as I waited patiently for my orders to report to the Replacement Center.

10

California, Here I Come

Louise and I developed a plan. This was the plan: one, Louise would research hotels in San Francisco and decide which one she would stay in while waiting to hear further from me. Two, she would research the best way for her to get to San Francisco—train, plane or bus; San Francisco because that's where most of the troop ships went. Three, I would find out all I could about my return—when and where. Four, she would arrange things with her job whereby she could leave on short notice. We worked on this plan over and over again for weeks before I knew anything about the Army's plans for me.

In the meantime, Louise's dad offered to take her with him to the National Homebuilders Association Convention in Chicago. (Chicago in the middle of January didn't sound like much fun to me.) She was excited, because friends we had made when we were stationed at Fort Lee—Janie and Irving Joel from Richmond, VA—had moved to Chicago, and they invited Louise to stay with them. The more I tried to find out the "when" and "where" of my return, the more frustrated I got. It looked like the first part of February to San Francisco or Seattle by ship—maybe by plane. Less probable possibilities: eastward to Hawaii, then through the Panama Canal to New York; or westward to Australia, Thailand, India, Suez Canal, Turkey, Greece, France, England, New York. Some GIs were actually sent by way of that route, dropping off UN troops along the way. With the Army, you never knew.

◆　　　◆　　　◆

I received a call from a Mr. Leroy Williams. He said he was with the CIC. That was the intelligence agency that dealt with U.S. armed forces' involvement in illegal activities, as opposed to the CIA, which dealt with foreign intelligence and espionage.

"Lieutenant, I need to talk to you about a case I am working on. May I send a jeep to pick you up?" Williams asked in a very soft voice.

"Okay," I responded, and he set the time.

The driver was a young Korean woman, wearing tight-fitting khaki slacks and a black sweater. She took me to a nondescript little house on the outskirts of Pusan. Mr. Williams lived and worked there. He gave me a matter-of-fact welcome as he, looking at the floor, led me to his office. He was smoking a pipe, which was sending out a pleasant aroma, wore plain-looking civilian clothes, and as we entered his office he established his credentials. The case involved a U.S. Army Warrant Officer. (Warrant Officers ranked above enlisted men and below commissioned officers and usually had been in the service a long, long time). W. O. Smith (not his real name) had been arrested and was being held without charges by the Korean Police in Kwangju, the largest town in the southwest corner of the peninsula.

"Lieutenant, I need you to go to Kwangju, investigate the Smith case, negotiate his release and bring him back to Pusan."

I questioned, "Why me? This sounds more like law enforcement work for the Military Police rather than pre-trial defense."

He responded, "Lieutenant, I selected you after careful consideration. You know your way around that part of Korea. You have had successful negotiations with the people and know how they think. You're experienced in pre-trial defense work and have the required security clearance."

"This case is too sensitive for a novice. I've cleared this matter with the 32nd Group commander and Captain Rucker, who is sending Lt. Dortch down from Teagu during your absence."

Figure 46—Lt John Dortch at the UNMC

Rucker, by the way, was a changed man. He learned to like Search and Recovery work; it gave him a sense of worth and accomplishment. He asked that I call him "Paul" instead of Captain Rucker. Plus, he started going with a cute-looking DOD civilian. The two of them would fly down to Pusan every week or two to spend the night at the Tongnae Springs Resort.

I was full of questions, such as "How am I going to get there? Is anyone going with me? How long do you think this will take? I'm actually waiting for my orders to go stateside."

"There is no suitable helicopter available. Use your jeep and Captain Yon as your interpreter. The round trip should not take more than six or seven days. It is a day-and-a-half to two-day drive, allowing you at least two days to negotiate Smith's release. Time is important here. I'd like you to report to me here tomorrow at 0700, ready to go."

Williams didn't leave me much choice. Captain Yon and I got everything ready and met Mr. Williams at 0700. He handed me the Smith file, information on how I could contact the CIC agent in Kwangju, and a packet filled with Won (Korean money), along with instructions for accounting for disbursements.

"Lieutenant, you'll understand a lot more about this case after you read the file. The Won is for negotiation purposes; the Korean authorities will surely want money. I'll see you when you get back. Good luck."

Captain Yon and I headed toward Masan, where I planned to have lunch and see some friends. Our first stop was Kim's school. He came running out and gave me a big hug. When I told him where I was going he begged to go with me, but I had to tell him he couldn't.

When Captain Yon and I went back to the jeep after lunch, Kim was in the back seat with a great big smile on his face.

We made it to the missionary's compound before dark—the same missionaries that came to my rescue when one of the S&R Teams blew two tires back in the spring. They were happy to see me and I was happy to see them. When I told them we were headed to Kwangju, they insisted it would be better to stay with them, have dinner, spend the night, and get an early start in the morning. That way we would avoid any nighttime driving. They explained that there was still some guerilla activity in the area, despite the concentrated efforts of the ROK Army since the cease fire to eliminate them. Since we had the time, the missionaries gave us a tour of the entire compound. It was surprisingly well-developed and spread out over several acres. There was a school, a hospital, and a chapel. They had their own vegetable garden, pig pen, chicken yard and duck pond.

That night I had the opportunity to read the Smith file. The CIC had been watching Smith for several months, ever since he had applied for and received a back-to-back tour in Korea. It seemed that Smith was involved in an illegal currency exchange operation which had engaged in converting U.S. Military script into Korean Won, then to U.S. Greenbacks. Suspicions heightened when the CIC learned that he had headed toward southwest Korea. The UN had no military presence there and was off limits to U.S. personnel because of the guerilla activity.

When we arrived in Kwangju, Captain Yon called the CIC agent, who as it turned out was simply a low-level Korean contact agent in the southwestern region. The agent gave us directions to our quarters and to the police station where W.O. Smith was being held. Kwangju was a crowded, but clean (comparatively speaking) town, with a decided Chinese influence. There were several banks, which explained why W.O. Smith went there in the first place. The Korean police chief was very polite to us. We spent at least an hour discussing things like our drive from Pusan, my work, Captain Yon's position, and Kim's story. I think Kim's being there helped set a wholesome and unarming affect. Finally, we got to the matter of W.O. Smith. Even though he never mentioned why he had arrested Smith, the chief made it sound like Smith was the most notorious criminal he had ever encountered and his release would put the entire country at great risk. But then it didn't take long for the chief to mention the fact that it had cost him considerable Won to provide his prisoner with food, lodging, and other services. We picked up on that and started negotiating on "how much." It did not take too long to arrive at an acceptable amount. After I handed the Won to the Chief, he sent his deputies to get W.O Smith.

I recognized him! He had spent a lot of time in Masan at the Top-of-the-Mark. Even though he wasn't a commissioned officer, they let him play poker and gin rummy in the high-stakes games. What a character—real out-going and entertaining.

The drive back to Pusan was uneventful. Smith talked non-stop and told one dirty joke after another. We spent the night with the missionaries, dropped Kim off in Masan, and delivered W.O. Smith to Mr. Williams, who arrested Smith on the spot, charging him with illegal currency exchange violations exceeding $250,000. Wow! Was I glad to be finished with that assignment!

◆   ◆   ◆

My orders to report to the Replacement Center were waiting for me at the 114th HQ. It was a simple matter for me to go across the road every morning, check in, look at the rotation list for my assignment, and return to the 114th. This process could go on for a week or more. I took the time to decide what to pack for my return and get ready to leave.

I soon became overwhelmed with the "farewells." The men of the 114th organized a special night at the Non-Commissioned Officers' (NCO) Club in my honor. They arranged extraordinary entertainment and invited everybody from outside the 114th they thought I'd like to share the evening with, like the liaisons from the various countries with whom I had worked. The next morning, Mr. Lee, with all the Korean employees, gathered together and with gracious ceremony presented me with a beautiful black lacquer box with inlaid mother-of-pearl designs. Inside the lid was inscribed, "To Lt. Pailet from Korean employee." Captain Yon gave me an authentic, traditional silver barrette that the Korean women used when they wore their hair in a bun. The Ethiopian liaison gave me the beautiful brass insignia off of his cap. The center of the insignia had a lion, which depicted King Solomon, and above the lion was a Star of David.

Kim came from Masan and pleaded to spend the remaining time with me. He was with me when my name appeared on the list. It was very emotional. I was not prepared for that. Up until that moment I had handled the good-byes and the gifts like an officer. But the total reality of my leaving for good did not engulf me until that moment, when Kim, with tears rolling down his cheeks, pulled a picture of himself out of his pocket. On the rear he had written, "I'm going to miss you, Pop. Love, Kim."

To be candid, a month or so earlier I had entertained the notion of bringing Kim to the States after my return in order to give him a good education. I learned that the only way to do that would be for Louise and me to begin the daunting process invented by the Army to discourage marriages and adoptions—ultimately, in this case, requiring a legal adoption. When I worked up the nerve to introduce the subject by letter to our families, the response was sympathetic and compassionate, but realistic. The issue of race was insurmountable. Most Americans, especially Southerners, had never seen a Korean. There would surely be xenophobia. It would not be fair to Kim. I did not pursue the idea.

Figure 47—Kim in new winter clothes Louise sent

Figure 48—Kim with THP's Swagger Stick

◆   ◆   ◆

I received my assignment. I was to be the troop ship's bursar. This meant that before sailing, each GI would come to my desk and give me all of his Military Script. I was responsible for counting, recording, and turning in the total. Then while at sea, I would receive the total amount in U.S. greenbacks and reverse the process. There were over one thousand GIs on that ship, so it was quite a job. Fortunately, it only took a few days and it was over. Happily, my books balanced. Some of the other officers had assignments that kept them busy the entire sixteen days it took us to go from Pusan to Seattle.

The deck was packed with GIs as the troopship pulled out of the bustling Pusan Harbor. It didn't take long for each of us to notice how different the air was. One GI asked, "What's that strange odor?"

Another GI answered, "Fresh air! Don't you remember what it smelled like?"

Guess what? I was going to Seattle and Louise was going to San Francisco, a thousand miles away.

I learned the ship's destination from a member of the crew with whom I became friendly while spending time on the upper deck. Even though the upper deck was ordinarily off-limits to all GIs, they let me spend time there because I had completed my assignment and the seas had become rough. There were many on board who was very sea sick, and the circulation of air down below was hardly adequate. In fact, it was horrible down there. Thankfully, my friend even arranged for me to have my meals in the crew's officers' dining room.

In order to help overcome my own sickness, I spent as much time as I could out on the deck. Even though it was bitter cold, the fresh air was a welcome relief. I braced myself, got comfortable, gazed at the endless expanse of the angry-looking sea and sky and let my feelings direct my thoughts. My thoughts focused on Louise. From the time I met the train in Tuscaloosa at the start of my junior and Louise's freshman year and helped her with her luggage until we said good-bye at the airport in New Orleans, we were like, as they say, "Siamese twins." We spent so much time together we thoroughly knew each other and we shared many wonderful experiences. Our love was solid. However, after such an event-filled year with all the many exotic experiences, I realized I must be a different person than when we were last together. What would Louise be like? She certainly had her unique experiences without me. She, too, must have changed in some ways. How? Regardless, I was confident we would quickly readjust to each other. It was not something I worried about, but it did make for interesting thinking.

I reflected on our wedding and our honeymoon trip. The wedding ceremony took place at the Vine Street Temple located on 7th Avenue (formerly Vine Street) in downtown Nashville. Rabbi William B. Silverman officiated. We had seven pairs of bridesmaids and groomsmen. That was August 14, 1951. It was 100 degrees and there was no air-conditioning. My brother Lester was my best man and Louise's cousin Sarah Ann was her maid-of-honor. The lavish wedding reception took place. at the Woodmont Country Club. We observed all of the traditional rituals of cutting the cake, with Louise smearing the icing in my face, throwing the bridal bouquet and the garter. After the reception we changed into our "going away clothes" with everybody throwing rice at us as we ran to the car that was waiting to whisk us off to our secret wedding night location.

The next morning Louise's dad drove us to the airport, where we flew to Mexico City We stayed at the Reforma Hotel the first week, then flew to Acapulco for the second week. There we stayed at the just-built Calleta Beach Hotel, right on the ocean at the southern tip of gorgeous Calleta Beach.

Both places were thoroughly enjoyable. They were different from any place either of us had ever been. We found Mexico City cosmopolitan, with very sophisticated supper clubs featuring elaborate floor shows and guitar music throughout the evening. I knew someone who lived there—a man named Octavio Horcasitas. He was in the sugar business and had visited in New Orleans on business trips. We had a mutual friend who had introduced us. Octavio told me to be sure and call him when Louise and I got to the city. We did. He met us and he and his wife took us to an upscale, authentic Mexican restaurant where we were introduced to *paella*. The next day they took us to see and climb ancient pyramids on the outskirts of the city. On our own, Louise and I went to the bull fights. In Mexico the Matador kills the bull—that is if the bull doesn't kill him first. There was a full afternoon of fights, one after the other. It was sort of like going to the race track, except for the gushing blood and the removal of the dead bull between fights. Louise turned green and it took several days to get her color back.

Acapulco was very resort-like. We met Candy Reynolds on the beach one day and became friends. She was a famous pin-up girl during World War II. She was known for wearing polka dot bikinis. Pin-up posters showing a scantily-dressed girl in a provocative pose were very popular with the GI's. Marilyn Monroe was the most famous of all…in the pose showing her dress being blown up by the wind. Candy invited us to go with her and her Mexican boy friend, Chi Chi Rodriguez, to Jai Lai one night. We had never heard of Jai Lai before and were absolutely amazed at the display of skill and athleticism of the players. We also learned how to bet on the player or team you hoped would win the next game. Another night we went with Candy and Chi Chi to the hotel supper club that was located at the top of a high cliff overlooking the Pacific Ocean. During dinner we watched daring divers perform beautiful swan dives, one after the other, off the edge of the precipice. They dove into the rough waters in the narrow cove two hundred or so feet below. They had to time their dive so they entered the water in between waves in order to avoid being crushed against the rocks. Chi Chi, as it turned out, was the featured diver. When it was time for the last and most daring dive, Chi Chi got up from our dinner table, went outside, removed his clothes except for his diving trunks, climbed up on the diver's perch, studied the waves, and performed a spectacular triple forward flip in the tuck position. There was a standing ovation as he returned to the table for coffee and dessert.

Fun!

Naturally, I was excited about what promised to be a second honeymoon trip. Our plan included stays in San Francisco, Los Angeles, and Las Vegas. Would we be able to pull this off? Upon arrival in Seattle, the Army was going to present me with orders, informing me where and when I must go in order to be discharged from active duty. I was hoping for at least two weeks, but with the Army one never knew.

I spent quite a bit of time thinking about the past year in Korea. What was the war all about? What, if anything, did the war accomplish? Was it worth the more than two million soldiers and civilians being killed and maimed, the disrupted lives and the billions of dollars? Tough questions—no sure answer—one could only express a feeling, a belief, a theory. I felt that the war was worth the effort. I believed that had President Truman decided to let the North Koreans invade and occupy the south without resistance, the results would have been far worse. Not only would the Communists have slaughtered every businessman and his family, slaughtered everyone whom they even thought opposed them, but it would have emboldened the Communists everywhere to advance their cause, which seemed to be World domination. Until Korea, Communism had been spreading without serious opposition. My theory was that Communism was a real and present threat to the USA and the western world. I was proud of Truman and Eisenhower, as well as the generals and admirals who led the UN Forces in stopping the Communist attempt to take over the South. Early on, General MacArthur wanted to keep going and finish the job. After all, we were the only country with the atomic bomb. Instead of following MacArthur's plan, Truman fired and replaced him.

My main thought on Communism, which we had studied at Newman School, was that Communism was against human nature. The whole idea of "from each according to his ability—to each according to his needs" simply did not make any convincing sense to me, but I could understand the appeal—too good to be true. The law of the jungle made more sense to me. To me, for a society to prosper there must be competition at all levels and reward for those who were successful; there must be incentives for people to get up in the morning, eager to do a good job. And there must be an environment that encourages wholesome family life and spiritual fulfillment.

I reflected on the many discussions Harry Martin and I had had about politics and religion (the two subjects they say not to talk about). I tried to analyze my own positions. How could I be a political conservative, but at the same time a religious liberal? It seemed like a contradiction. I concluded that the common denominator was individual freedom—self-determination. I associated left-leaning political systems and fundamentalist religions with restrictions on personal liberties and control by those in power. So in my own mind, I felt I was consistent.

I gave thought to what I would be doing after I mustered out of the army and into civilian life and the work force. I looked forward greatly to being reunited with Louise, my parents and my brother Lester. My plan was to help my dad in his jewelry business. Even though he was a wonderful, highly-skilled jeweler and a super salesman, he had no formal education in the office and business departments. I felt I had received a good business education at Alabama, especially for small business, and I was eager to make my contribution to Pailet & Penedo, Inc.

◆   ◆   ◆

On the sixteenth day, we pulled into the Seattle harbor, where we were greeted by a cheering crowd and a brass band. Processing did not take terribly long. I received my orders to report to Camp Chaffe in Fort Smith, Arkansas, two weeks hence, to be processed for discharge from active duty and to receive my reserve unit assignment. (In order to receive my ROTC commission I had to sign an agreement to serve two years of active duty and two years in the Reserves.)

Figure 49—Welcoming cheers at Seattle pier

Upon arrival at the processing center, the first thing I did was to call Louise's parents to find out where Louise was and to assure them that I was fine. I called the St. Francis Hotel in San Francisco. There was no answer in her room, so I left a message with the operator. "I am in Seattle and will get a flight to San Francisco as soon as I can." I spoke to my mother, my dad, and my brother. It was a thrilling experience after so many months, a relief to know first hand that they were fine and to know it wouldn't be long before we were together again.

During the processing in Seattle, I was with a group of Air Force officers who, lucky for me, were flying an Air Force plane to San Francisco from Seattle that afternoon. They included me on the flight (in other words, I "hitched a ride") and I arrived in San Francisco in record time. As we entered the Terminal building I spotted Louise. Obviously, she had no intention of waiting for me to call the hotel to say I had arrived at the airport. She was wearing a smart-looking navy blue suit, a hat and gloves—an indescribable, stunning sight to me. Happy tears welled up in our eyes. We embraced for the longest time before either of us could say anything.

Figure 50—Louise in San Francisco, wearing Ethiopian Insignia

Epilogue

It is now 2004, 50 years since.

Louise and I enjoyed our second honeymoon. We started in San Francisco, then flew to Los Angeles and Las Vegas. In Vegas we stayed in the brand new Sands Hotel. (That same hotel was demolished earlier this year because of obsolescence.) From Las Vegas we flew to Fort Smith, Arkansas, where I was separated from active duty at Camp Chaffe. After visiting family and friends in Nashville and other places in the South, we settled in New Orleans, where I joined my dad, David "Dewey" in Pailet & Penedo, Inc. and where, nine months after my return, our first child, Patricia Louise, was born. I soon realized that the jewelry business was not for me and I was not for it. I did not have the talent or the appreciation for designing or crafting jewelry. Neither was I interested in studying gemology, as did my brother Lester, who was so good at it. This made it especially difficult for me to sell to the public. I did not like the confinement—six days a week (seven at Christmas time), gulping down meals and not getting home until nine or ten o'clock during the busy seasons. After Patricia was born, Louise and I moved to Nashville, where I joined her dad Albert in the land development and construction business.

Our second child, Albert David, was born in 1957, and our third, Toby Lynn, was born in 1963. At the age of 36 (1966) I enrolled in a night law school, which was especially designed for students who worked full-time and who had families. Four years later I was admitted to the Tennessee Bar and began practicing law in connection with the real estate and construction business.

During these past 50 years, Louise and I have experienced triumphs and tragedies, the details of which need not be set out here except for a brief sketch of the current status of our immediate family.

Our son, Al, is married to Janet. They have two sons: Marshall, 17, and Edward, 15. They live in the upper west side of Manhattan. Al practices law with a prestigious Park Avenue law firm. Janet has her own consulting firm. Marshall has had several roles on Broadway: the younger Von Trapp son in *The Sound of Music* for one. He composed the music for and Al wrote the book and lyrics for a musical comedy, *Swimming Upstream,* which has been produced and shown with full cast at a theater cabaret. Edward (Eddie) is multi-talented and is in the 10th grade at the Friends' Seminary in Manhattan.

Our daughter Toby is married to Gregg Silverstein. They have two daughters: Perri Dee, 10 and Sydney Lee, 9. They just moved into a gorgeous new home in Davie, FL. Gregg practices law with his brother and father in North Miami Beach; Toby is a full-time homemaker and mother. Perri and Sydney attend University School and are adorable, bright, beautiful and a pleasure to have as granddaughters.

Louise and I own two condominiums: one in Nashville and one in Fort Lauderdale. We alternate seasonally between the two. Like they say, "*Somebody* has to do it!"

We have maintained friendships with many of those who took part in this story. As mentioned in the Introduction, Harry Martin, Joe Bernstein, Albert Mintz, Fred Rosenberg and Ann Silberman have read this work. We see each of them somewhat regularly when circumstances permit and have shared joys and sorrows with each.

Shortly after we settled in Nashville, Louise and I helped two Koreans who needed sponsorship in order to do graduate work in an American university. They were Hain Pack Lee, Harry Martin's interpreter, and Sun Moon Khang, who interpreted for me briefly, but whom I knew very well. They flew from Seoul to Nashville. Neither had ever been in a supermarket nor driven on a modern highway. They stayed with us, to the delight of our children, and I arranged for them to work as laborers on one of our construction jobs to toughen them up, improve their English, and allow them to earn some money before school started.

As far as keeping up with members of the 114th QM GR Company, we did exchange Christmas cards for several years with Ernie Modarelli, who married and had one child after another. We also kept up with Dick Priest, who also married and had one child after another. The only one I visited was Dick Priest. The visit took place while taking my son Al on an interview tour of colleges. Williams College was next on the itinerary. Dick lived in Kingston, NY, which was not terribly far out of the way. When I called to say that we'd be in the vicinity, he insisted that we come to his home for dinner, which we did. It was a sincere pleasure seeing him again, reminiscing about times in Korea and catching up on the past 20 years.

◆   ◆   ◆

In 1991, Louise and I celebrated our 40th wedding anniversary in Japan and Korea. We spent time in Tokyo, Hiroshima, Eta Jima, Pusan, Seoul, Masan, Chinhae, and drove around the Naktong River area.

Tokyo, of course, is a huge, modern world-class metropolis, and we had a very urbane visit. While on the island of Eta Jima we walked around the facilities where I had lived and studied 38 years previously. Most of the buildings were still there and were once again being used by the Japanese for the training of naval cadets. In Hiroshima, the Japanese had built a beautiful "Peace Park" surrounding the area of "Ground Zero." There is a modern museum devoted to the preservation and display of an overwhelming collection of items related to the atomic bomb explosion of 1945. Throughout the park there are beautiful and very meaningful sculptures, and the ruins of that reinforced concrete building which I visited in 1953. The Japanese preserved it as a permanent reminder of the awesome force unleashed by that bomb. While walking through the park, Louise and I were approached by school children, eager to talk to Americans, not only to practice their English, but to interview us for use in a class. They asked many interesting and relevant questions, but mainly wanted to know our opinions and attitudes about the use of atomic bombs on civilian populations.

Pusan had grown into a huge, bustling city; it even has a subway system. We stayed at a modern resort hotel in Hyundae Beach, which was developed on the site of the K-9 Airport. Hyundae Beach fronts on the body of water separating Korea from Japan. The Japanese and most maps refer to that body of water as "The Sea of Japan." However, the Koreans still refer to it as "The East Sea." There are no signs of the Koreans forgiving the Japanese for those thirty-five years of harsh occupation.

The very first day in Pusan, Louise and I took a taxi to the United Nations Military Cemetery. It had been turned over to an international commission, which has done a reasonably good job of maintaining the facilities. They charge an admission fee, and it appeared to host a steady trickle of visitors. We located the man in charge. It turned out that he had been a young employee at the time I was there. He was most pleased to show us around and go through the old records which dated back to 1953 and 1954. He even found orders and other documents that I had signed.

We hired a driver to take us to the Masan area. On the way, we drove on a beautiful controlled access highway—first, through Chinhae, the town where I went to Mr. Lee's grandchild's first birthday party. We found that famous monument right there in the center of the "old" part of town. On the way to Masan we drove through the tunnel that had been built by U.S. POWs of the Japanese during World War II.

Masan, naturally, had grown and modernized. We went up the hill to the site of "The Top of the Mark." On the site is a beautiful high-rise hotel, The Shilla. We had lunch (fried butterfly shrimp) at the roof-top restaurant, which had a panoramic view of Masan and its harbor. I did not recognize the harbor facilities. They had been updated to accommodate containerized shipping with huge modern cranes. While Louise was shopping in the gift shop, I took the time to stare out over Masan and reflect on the months I had lived and worked there. The experience helped refresh my memory on many of the details I have incorporated in this memoir.

I thought about Kim and wondered what ever happened to him. After I returned to the States, we exchanged one or two letters, but for whatever reason, we did not continue to write. Another U.S. Army lieutenant had taken up where I left off. Louise and I took his picture with us and asked several people to help us locate him, but we were unable to find any trace of him.

My mind was boggled by the city of Seoul, which had just hosted the summer Olympics. The last time I was there the city was in total ruins. Now it was one of the major cities of the world—the capitol of one of the important democratic countries of Asia and one of the economic miracles of history. To think that those kids I saw walking along those pot-holed rural roads, throwing their pencils, rulers and notebooks in front of my jeep just to see what would happen, were now building and selling automobiles, TV's and electronics to us and hiring *our* sons and daughters to work for *them*.

It did my heart and mind good to see the phenomenal progress and prosperity that had taken place in South Korea over the past 50 years. This happened in an open, capitalistic, democratic society. Of course, the USA helped. But, the Soviet Union and Communist China provided help to The People's Republic of North Korea. Unfortunately, North Korea is still a closed, totalitarian, Communistic society—a hermit state—with people suffering from malnutrition; it is a failed, angry, poor, sad state.

Unfortunately, not much, if anything, has changed in relationships between North and South Korea, even though the spread of Communism is no longer a threat. The border between the countries is still closed, and opposing armies are still sitting on ready, just like in 1954. And when someone shoots a duck above the Han River and the duck falls on one side or the other, the duck belongs to the one on that side of the river.

0-595-33433-4

7040649R00080

Made in the USA
San Bernardino, CA
21 December 2013